COVER UP—OR UNCANNY TRUTH?

"Are you saying that the Navy tried to make you invisible, in some sort of experiment?"

"Electronic camouflage," came the answer. "Some sort of electrical camouflage produced by pulsating energy fields.... We couldn't take it—none of us. Though it affected us in different ways. Some only saw double, others began to laugh and stagger like they were drunk, and a few passed out. Some even claimed that they had passed into another world and had seen and *talked* to strange alien beings. And in some cases the effects weren't temporary. I was told later that several had died.... But as for the rest of us who survived—well, they just let us go. Disability, they called it. Discharged as mentally unbalanced and unfit for further service.... That way, if the Navy ever got questioned about it, they could just chalk it up as a story cooked up by a bunch of nuts...."

THE PHILADELPHIA EXPERIMENT

A bizarre excursion into the unknown

William L. Moore is an English and French teacher in the Minnesota school system, a playwright, author, and an investigator of the unexplained. His collaboration with Charles Berlitz on *The Philadelphia Experiment* has taken him on investigations throughout the United States during the past four years. Moore lives in Minnesota with his wife and three children. His initial interest in the Philadelphia Experiment stems from a meeting with Charles Berlitz while Berlitz was on a lecture tour.

Charles Berlitz, the author of *The Bermuda Triangle*, is a renowned linguist, lecturer, and underwater explorer. In addition to *The Bermuda Triangle*, which has sold over 10 million copies in twenty-three languages, Berlitz has written other best sellers on archaeology, languages, Atlantis, and underwater exploration. He lives in Florida, from where he is continuing his research on the Bermuda Triangle.

The Philadelphia Experiment

PROJECT INVISIBILITY

An Account of a Search for a
Secret Navy Wartime
Project That May Have Succeeded—Too Well

by William L. Moore

in consultation with

Charles Berlitz

FAWCETT CREST • NEW YORK

Dedicated to the outriders of science whose quest for knowledge takes them to the most distant
stars and to the innermost worlds.

CONTENTS

When a distinguished but elderly scientist states that something is possible, he is almost certainly right. When he states that something is impossible, he is probably wrong.

—Arthur C. Clarke

Actually the biggest deterrent to scientific progress is a refusal of some people, including scientists, to believe that things that seem amazing can really happen.

—George S. Trimble (of Glenn L. Martin Co. 1955; and later, director of NASA Manned Spacecraft Center, Houston)

The
Philadelphia
Experiment

Introduction
by Charles Berlitz

During my research for the writing of *The Bermuda Triangle* I came across an incident so unusual in terms of accepted scientific possibility as to be almost incredible. In earlier ages, perhaps, it would doubtlessly have been easier to believe, but only as a manifestation of pure magic—the work of wizards. For the alleged incident concerned nothing less than a successful experiment in invisibility, performed in 1943 in the decidedly unmagical surroundings of the Philadelphia Navy Yard.

According to one version of this incident, a Navy destroyer escort was caused, by a series of magnetic manifestations, to vanish temporarily and then to reappear *at another place*. More detailed versions tell of deleterious effects on crew members who manned the disappearing craft and whose psychological aftereffects and in some instances deaths caused further experimentation to be abandoned.

This incident, story, or legend has been consistently denied by the Office of Naval Information but nevertheless appears to have a persistent and ever-expanding life through references in print and insistent declarations of individuals (who generally are unwilling to be named) who claim to have witnessed the events which now, for want of a better (or code) name, are referred to as the "Philadelphia Experiment."

My own special interest in the Philadelphia Experiment was connected with the possibility that a shift in the molecular composition of matter, induced by intensified and resonant magnetism, could cause an object to vanish— one possible explanation of some of the disappearances within the Bermuda Triangle. In my lectures throughout the nation and overseas I noted an extraordinary public interest when I mentioned the Philadelphia Experiment, and, surprisingly, occasionally there appeared a "witness," who usually had a passion for anonymity.

During a college lecture appearance two years ago I met a young English teacher, an author with a flair for research. His obsessive interest in the Philadelphia Experiment story has taken him to various parts of the country, and his dedication has helped him to overcome official denials, to locate conveniently missing documents, to renew the memory of forgetful witnesses, and even to find certain key scientists whose proximity to and familiarity with this experiment "which never took place" had impelled them to live quietly in an extremely isolated area, perhaps for reasons of health (or survival).

This new research unearthed by Bill Moore, the tireless researcher referred to above, has been incorporated into the following joint investigation which presents information never before revealed; information which strangely indicates that the "impossible" experiment actually took place. The research itself is a fascinating exercise in overcoming official inertia, camouflage, and cover-up. The inference is extraordinary, for if the experiment was carried on as indicated, we once stood, and perhaps still stand, at the edge of the discovery of how to make objects and people, others and ourselves, invisible—one of the oldest dreams of man.

But this and other ancient dreams no longer seem so unattainable, especially since 1945, when a dream of supreme and explosive power first became an actuality at Alamogordo. Coincidentally, at least two other projects more properly reserved to the domain of science fiction were reportedly under way at a time (1943) when America was seeking unusual aids for protection and survival. One of these was concerned with antigravity and the other with invisibility, but work on these was reportedly suspended with the evident success of the atom bomb.

This unusual book makes a surprisingly concrete case for the actuality of this experiment in invisibility. At the same time one might consider the premise that the most remarkable discoveries of science should not necessarily be triggered by wartime conditions—an example being the peaceful exploration of space.

If the Philadelphia Experiment was stopped at the edge of success, one feels that perhaps it should be started again or continued. For, as the universe expands around us, we cannot remain at a standstill in our efforts to unlock the cosmic secrets of matter, space, and time.

CHAPTER 1

A Close Encounter with the Incredible

The area around Colorado Springs is particularly beautiful at all times of the year, but especially so in the late summer when the heat of the day is tempered by cool nights and the skies sometimes have an almost crystal clarity. It was on one such evening in 1970 that two airmen, James Davis of Maryland and Allen Huse of Texas, lacking anything in particular to do, set out with a camera for a refreshing walk in nearby War Memorial Park. The air was warm and pleasant, and as dusk came on, Huse began to occupy himself with taking photographs of the moon. Davis strolled around the park, enjoying the welcome break from the routine at nearby Colorado Springs Air Force Base, where both men had been stationed for some months.

A moment later, Davis was suddenly approached by a rather strange-looking man whom he had noticed earlier hanging around the War Memorial monument—a short, balding, somewhat unkempt fellow. He recalls noticing that the man had a sort of faraway look in his eyes. Davis' initial reaction was that he was about to be asked for a handout. But a surprise was in store for him.

"Notice you're in the Air Force," the man said. "How do you like it?"

Davis responded that he got along all right, but that he sometimes wished the routine weren't so rigorous. "Not enough time to relax," he said.

The man agreed.

One thing led to another and soon the two were busy exchanging stories.

"You know," said the small man, "I was an officer once. Navy—during the war. But they did things to me. Finally put me out to pasture. Crazy, they say." He tapped the side of his head lightly with a finger. "But I'm not, you know. It was that experiment that did it. Couldn't take the pressure, so they put me out."

He pulled out a wallet and flashed a worn and obviously outdated ID card. "See?" he said. "Navy, just like I said."

Davis was curious. "Experiment?" he said. "Just what sort of an experiment are you talking about?"

The answer stunned him.

"Invisibility," said the man. "It was when they were trying to make a ship invisible. It would have been perfect camouflage if it had worked. And it did, too! With the ship, that is.

But those of us on board . . . well, it didn't work too well on us. We couldn't stand the effects of the energy field they were using. It did things to us. I should never have taken that assignment up to Philadelphia. It was Top Secret. I could've backed out, but I didn't. If I'd had any idea what I was getting myself into, I sure as hell would have told them where to get off."

Davis was beginning to wonder whether he was hearing what he thought he was.

"Just what are you talking about?" he wanted to know. "Are you saying that the Navy tried to make you invisible, in some sort of experiment, or what?"

"Electronic camouflage," came the answer. "Some sort of electrical camouflage produced by pulsating energy fields. I don't know exactly what sort of energy they were using, but there was sure a lot of it. We couldn't take it—none of us. Though it affected us in different ways. Some only saw double, others began to laugh and stagger like they were drunk, and a few passed out. Some even claimed that they had passed into another world and had seen and *talked* to strange alien beings. And in some cases the effects weren't temporary. I was told later that several had died. Anyhow, I never saw them again. But as for the rest of us—those of us who survived—well, they just let us go. Disability, they called it. Discharged as mentally unbalanced and unfit for further service. Pensioned off!" he said bitterly.

"But why?" asked Davis.

By this time, Huse, who had overheard snatches of this strange conversation from several yards away, came over and joined the pair. Davis introduced his friend and they shook hands.

"Glad to meet you," said the man.

After the brief introduction, Davis pursued his point.

"You mean," he said, "that the Navy discharged all these men as mental incompetents because the experiment failed?"

"That's correct," said their mysterious companion. "That's exactly what they did. Of course, they put us away for a few months before they did it. To 'rest up,' they said. Also, to try to convince us that it had never happened, I think. Anyway, in the end they swore us to secrecy— even though nobody's likely to believe such a story anyway. How about you? You're in the Air Force; do you believe it? Do you believe what I'm telling you?"

"I don't know," Davis replied. "I certainly agree that it's a fantastic story. Almost too fantastic. I just don't know."

"Well, it's true just the same. Every damn word of it. Of course, that's exactly why they discharged us as mentally unfit. In case anybody ever thought about believing it, I mean. That way, if the Navy ever got questioned about it, they could just chalk it up as a story cooked up by a bunch of nuts. You've got to admit, it's a smart move from a security standpoint. Who's going to believe a certified looney? Anyway, that's my story."

The two airmen exchanged glances, and Huse rolled his eyes a bit. But before they could decide just how to react to this bizarre confidence, their companion had changed his topic to something more mundane and was busy making predictions about sunspots and the weather.

An hour or so later, they left him and headed back to the base. It was already quite dark and the coolness of a Colorado evening was beginning to penetrate their uniforms.

Even though they never saw this strange little man again, Davis and Huse discussed his bizarre tale several times over the course of the next few months. Huse, who had heard only a part of the man's story, was the more skeptical of the two, but both wondered whether there was really anything to this odd character they had met in the park, or whether he really was crazy. Eventually Davis was discharged and Huse was transferred, and they lost track of each other.

Several years later, in January 1978, Davis happened to pick up a paperback copy of Charles Berlitz' *The Bermuda Triangle* and was startled to read an account of the so-called Philadelphia Experiment, in which the Navy had allegedly made a destroyer escort and its crew invisible through the use of force fields during World War II. The conversation with the strange little man flooded back into his mind. After pondering it for several days, he finally decided to write Berlitz in care of his publisher and tell his story. Later, in a telephone interview with Moore, Davis identified Huse as the friend who had been with him, but said that he had no idea of Huse's whereabouts, since he had not seen him since he had left the Air Force. He believed, he said, that if Huse could be found, he would surely remember the conversation in the park and thus corroborate the story.

A week later, Moore succeeded in locating Davis' former friend and telephoned him. Huse was indeed able to confirm the basic facts of Davis' story. He recalled having been with Davis when they met the stranger in the park, as well as having discussed this character several times thereafter over a beer or two; but he was fuzzy on details of just what the man had told them.

"That was quite a few years ago," he said. "I don't really recall just what the man spoke about. There were some really strange things, though."

"Might he have made reference to having been involved in some sort of a Navy experiment project in Philadelphia?" Moore asked.

"Yes," replied Huse after a moment's thought. "Yes, I seem to remember that he claimed this. He said quite a few crazy things—I don't recall the details exactly—but I do seem to remember something about an experiement. I can also remember being pretty skeptical about what he said."

"But you don't recall the details?"

"No, not really. Davis might remember more than I can. He was the one who struck up the conversation in the first place."

"Have you seen or heard from Mr. Davis lately?"

"No, not since before I left the Air Force. That was sometime in June 1973." (Note: Davis had said that he had left Colorado Springs in August 1971.)

"Getting back to the man in the park, why do you think he picked you and your friend as the ones he wanted to tell his story to?"

"I don't know. I had the impression at the time that he had 'selected' us. We were there in uniform, and he kind of selected us, I guess. He seemed almost as if he wanted to get something off his chest and he wanted us to be the ones to hear it. We talked about this meeting several times at work and even mentioned it to some of our other friends. Everybody thought the whole thing was rather weird."

"You haven't any idea where this man might have come from or where he lived?"

"No. He showed up, and then more or less disappeared after that. I'm certain that I would have recognized him again if I had seen him around town, but I never did. We returned to that park quite a few times after that, too."

"Do you recall his mentioning anything about his discharge or having been injured by an experiment?"

"It seems to me that he may have said this was the reason for his discharge, but I'm not sure. There was something about an experiment, though. I'm sure of that."

Thus ended an interview that provided yet another piece of an already strange and mysterious puzzle which had been building for nearly thirty-five years and which even now is far from complete, and in fact may never be. Invisibility projects, men disappearing never to be heard from again, other men certified insane, references to "aliens" from space or another dimension—could some of these incredible but possibly related elements be essentially true?

One naturally hesitates to credit such reports and their sources. And yet, for over twenty years the rumors have persisted that the U.S. Navy, working under Top Secret conditions at the Philadelphia Navy Yard during World War II, succeeded in producing a powerful electronic force field which somehow got out of control and resulted in a ship's disappearance from sight and, some say, its subsequent "teleportation" from Philadelphia to Norfolk and back again in a matter of *seconds*.

Incredible? Yes...perhaps. But perhaps after all the evidence is in and examined, not quite so incredible after all. Investigations into the unexplained occasionally turn up things even more unusual than the original legend. This case was no exception.

CHAPTER 2

Fan Mail
for a Scientist

The Bermuda Triangle, Bigfoot monsters, UFOs, strange disappearances, ghosts and specters of all sorts and descriptions, psychic phenomena . . .all part of a continually growing list of happenings and events which, when anyone bothers to try to classify them, are inevitably placed somewhere in that netherworld between science and fantasy which is known as "the unexplained." Most readers, those with other and more pressing interests, content themselves with a shrug or a smile, and allow that at the very least an occasional excursion into the realm of the unknown is all very interesting—if for no other reason than for entertainment. Others, their minds hopelessly bedazzled and their judgment blinded by some inner need for truth, find themselves trapped by what began innocently enough as a passing interest.

The process inevitably commences with that peculiar brand of common curiosity which drives a once casually interested observer into trying to find a few answers on his own. Inevitably some strange story or other manages to pique inquisitive minds just enough to heighten the desire to solve a mystery, or at the very least to come up with a few more pertinent facts.

And so begins another of those hapless personal "investigations" which generally progress no further than a discussion with an interested friend, a few unanswered letters of inquiry, or perhaps some telephone calls which produce nothing by way of results but high telephone bills. But occasionally—just occasionally—fate steps in and allows the investigator to stumble upon a few facts which eventually become, almost without deliberate effort, the first forgings in the chain of a more fantastic story than was even dreamed of at the time the first inquiries were made.

As anyone who has ever gone in any depth into investigating the world of paranormal phenomena will vouch, there are numerous stories floating around on the fringe of believability which, though told, retold, and occasionally closely examined by investigators of psychic phenomena, never really make their way into public print, either because they are regarded as too fantastic to be believed or because it is thought that there isn't sufficient material to warrant a book-length treatment of the topic.

One of the most bizarre and incredible of these "borderland" stories, and one that has repeatedly popped up over the years without ever having received anything but the briefest of passing treatments in popular print, is that of the so-called Philadelphia Experiment. Although mentioned in books and articles by at least a dozen writers and researchers of the unexplained in the course of the past two decades, relatively little in the way of new material has been added to the original story, with the result that the tale has remained in a sort of suspended animation waiting for someone to make an in-depth investigation. Here, then, is one of the wildest tales ever to appear in what proposes to be a factual presentation—given along with the results of an intensive investigation which, ironically enough, began as an honest attempt on the part of the authors to explore and perhaps explode the myth.

The mystery begins with a scientist who at first glance appears to have been something of a mystery man in his own right. Nothing much is known about the early life of Morris Ketchum Jessup except a few bare facts. That he was a man of many and varied interests—scientist, astronomer, astrophysicist, mathematician, researcher, lecturer, author—is common knowledge, in spite of the fact that he was not the type to seek much publicity, or revel in it when he did get it. Named after his family's "rich uncle," a noted nineteenth-century railroad baron, financier, and philanthropist who gave his name to Cape Morris K. Jesup (*sic*), located on the northernmost tip of Greenland, Jessup was born in Rockville, Indiana, on March 20, 1900. Having turned the magic age of seventeen just weeks before this country's entrance into World War I, Jessup, like so many other young men his age, was caught up in the patriotic fervor, and his graduation from high school was virtually simultaneous with his enlistment in the U.S. Army. He was eventually to attain the rank of sergeant.

The war over, Jessup set about obtaining an education that would eventually lead to instructorships in astronomy and mathematics at Drake University, Des Moines, Iowa, and the University of Michigan at Ann Arbor. While a doctoral student at Michigan in the late 1920s, he seized an opportunity to travel to the Union of South Africa with a research team assigned to the University of Michigan's Lamont-Hussey Observatory in Bloemfontein, Orange Free State. While working with what was then the largest refracting telescope in the Southern Hemisphere, Jessup perfected a research program which resulted in the discovery of a number of physical double stars now catalogued by the Royal Astronomical Society in London.

Later, back in the States, he used these experiences as the basis for his doctoral dissertation in the field of astrophysics. Jessup finally completed and published this work in 1933, but it does not appear that he was ever actually awarded his Ph.D. Even so, many of those who knew him best chose to refer to him as Dr. Jessup, and it seems only fitting that we continue to do so.

During those depression years, at a time when many academicians were forced to earn their livings elsewhere because of an acute shortage of funds to pay professional salaries, Jessup was assigned by the U.S. Department of Agriculture as part of a team of scientists to go to Brazil to "study the sources of crude rubber in the headwaters of the Amazon." An odd assignment for an astronomer, but at least it was a job, and the work was interesting.

Following his return from the jungles, he signed on with the Carnegie Institute in Washington, D.C., as a photographer on an archaeological expedition which was being organized to study Mayan ruins in Central America. Jessup, it seems, was beginning to develop a taste for jungle exploration.

From Mexico he went on to explore the Inca and pre-Inca ruins of Peru. While he was there, he came to a startling conclusion. Upon observing the massive size of some of these stone ruins and the intricacy, exactness, and finesse of the construction techniques exployed, and considering the virtual impossibility that this sort of work could have been accomplished by hand without so much as the aid of a draft animal larger than the llama, Jessup, like Erich von

Daniken in later years (although with considerably less publicity), speculated that one possible explanation for these huge stone constructions was that, rather than having been constructed by the Incas, they were built in antediluvian times with the aid of levitating devices operated from sky ships of some sort. This was a rather unusual statement for anyone calling himself a scientist, and, needless to say, one hardly calculated to endear him to his colleagues. It makes Jessup one of the first proponents of what is now more than three decades later, the well-popularized "Ancient Astronauts" theory.

Putting scientific orthodoxy aside at grave peril to his academic career and reputation, Jessup continued to ponder the perplexing origins of these ancient Central and South American ruins, and in the early 1950s he undertook to continue his studies there at his own expense. It was during just such studies of ancient cultures on the high plateaus of Mexico that Jessup discovered a rather remarkable group of geologic formations which, upon closer examination, appeared to be a series of craters of some sort. There were at least ten of these, and they bore, he thought, certain remarkable similarities in structure and size to the mysterious lunar craters Linne and Hyginus N. Again going off on an unorthodox tangent for a scientist, Jessup, after completing a preliminary study of the matter, offered up his conclusion that they had been "made by objects from space." Commenting still further at a later date, he disclosed that he had discovered that the U.S. Air Force possessed a series of aerial photographs of these craters which had been taken by a reconnaissance plane operating with the permission of the Mexican government, but that these photos and the findings concerning them were being kept highly classified. Wishing to continue his own independent studies of these formations but having run short of money with which to finance the operation, Jessup was forced to return to the United States in 1954 in order to try to raise the necessary funds.

Having become interested in the flying-saucer phenomenon as it unfolded upon the American scene in the late 1940s and early 1950s—at first simply as a matter of personal curiosity and later from a more professional interest—Jessup began to sense connections between these possible "space ships" and his ancient ruins and mysterious craters. Firmly convinced that there had to be a solid scientific foundation for the phenomenon, and in pursuit of funds regardless of the source, he began to draw up a mental outline for a book which would, in his eyes, be the first truly "scientific" attempt to examine the UFO question on the basis of available historical evidence. UFOs (unidentified flying objects), he believed, had not only been with us for years, but could provide answers for many of the hitherto unexplained occurrences and events of history—including mysterious falls of ice, rocks, and even animals from the sky. Their means of operation was, he felt, by some as-yet-unrecognized principle of antigravity, and they appeared to be definitely of intelligent origin and design.

After moving to the Washington, D.C., area, Jessup began work on the book which had already taken shape in his mind—a work which would take a truly systematic look at a phenomenon he believed deserved serious scientific attention. He mounted a monumental research effort and labored throughout the summer, fall, and winter of 1954, and the work slowly began to take shape. It was finally complete and ready for the publisher on January 13, 1955. Entitling it *The Case for the UFO,* in the preface he characterized his work as "a serious attempt to bring order out of chaos, an attempt to pull all of the facets of this controversy into a basic stratum upon which to make an intelligent evaluation of the subject." Little did Jessup suspect that the publishing of this book by the Citadel Press in early 1955 would mark the beginning of an even more mysterious train of events that would remain the subject of intense controversy for years to come.

One of Jessup's prime areas of interest was the question of the motive power of UFOs. Time and again, both in his book and in his correspondence with friends and associates, he returned to this theme and to his belief that the earth had previously witnessed applications of this type of power in ancient or prehistoric times. An example of his thoughts on the topic is the following quotation from a letter to a correspondent dated December 20, 1954—when he was only weeks short of completing the final draft of his book: "The extension of the [UFO] motive-power theme to include some jolts to religion are rather obvious," he wrote. "This space race *could* be our *God*. They could have left the earth millennia ago."

A reliable source of motive power, he believed, was the all-important key to man's development; and until mankind could discover (or *re*discover) something more reliable than the "bully-brute" force of rocket power, he would be tied to the earth like a child to his mother's apron strings. That "something," in Jessup's mind, was the utilization of the universal gravitational field as a source of energy.

Jessup appealed both in print and in lectures to the public for serious research to be undertaken in this area of scientific endeavor, either by the government or by private individuals and corporations. Jessup's theories were to disturb at least one of his readers to such an extent that he began a correspondence wherein purportedly confidential Navy material and apparently bizarre imaginings were intermingled.

Even though *The Case for the UFO* never made the best-seller lists, it did manage to sell sufficient hardcover copies to warrant a Bantam paperback edition, which appeared in the early fall of 1955. It was not too long after the appearance of this paperback edition (most probably about mid-October) that Dr. Jessup received a rather strange letter. It came in the midst of a packet of the type of "fan mail" commonly generated by the publication of almost any book and which is routinely forwarded by publishers to their authors.

This particular letter, bearing a Pennsylvania postmark, was written in a rambling, scrawly hand in several different types and colors of pencil and pen, and in a very odd style. Capitalizations appeared in the midst of sentences, words were oddly used and misspelled, and punctuation, where employed at all, seemed almost to have been thrown in as some sort of afterthought. Entire phrases were frequently underscored in different colors of ink.

Even stranger than the appearance of the letter, however, was its content. Its author, it seems, was particularly interested in taking issue with certain of the references in Jessup's book dealing with the power of levitation (i.e., defying the force of gravity to lift heavy objects) as it was apparently known to the ancients, and went on to comment at some length that Jessup's guess concerning the use of same to build many ancient structures was essentially correct. Indeed, according to the letter writer, the power of levitation was not only scientifically possible, but had once been a "known process" here on Earth.

Unfortunately, no copies of this original letter seem to have survived, but we do know that the style of the letter was so convincing that Jessup wondered as he read it whether its author might by means of his strange writing style be trying to tell him that he personally possessed some firsthand knowledge of the process. The letter was signed "Carlos Miguel Allende."

Although unsure just how to take the whole thing, Jessup was apparently intrigued enough by the letter to take the time to send a brief response to the enigmatic Señor Allende asking that he supply more details.

Jessup at this point in his life was caught up in the rush of a heavy schedule, and after several months had slipped by without any additional word from his strange correspondent, he all but forgot about the affair. Busy with a series of public lectures and at the same time working to finish a second book entitled *UFO and the Bible* (the rush largely due to the maneuvers of his agents in New York who hoped to capitalize on the modest success of his first book), Jessup had little time to spend thinking about fan mail of any sort.

While traveling the lecture circuit he continued to impress upon the public the urgent need for some sort of government-sponsored research program in the area of antigravity. On occasion he even went so far as to tell his audiences that if they really wanted to help get the ball rolling they could contact their legislators about this "en masse." "If the money, thought, time, and energy now being poured uselessly into the development of rocket propulsion were invested in a basic study of gravity, beginning perhaps with continued research into Dr. Einstein's Unified Field concepts," he said, "it is altogether likely that we could have effective and economical space travel, at but a small fraction of the costs we are now incurring, within the next decade."

Unknown to Dr. Jessup, Allende appears to have been in the audience during at least one of these lectures, and what he heard caused him to write another most unusual letter.

On January 13, 1956, exactly one year to the day after his completion of the manuscript for *The Case for the UFO*, Jessup, now in Miami, was surprised to receive the following letter from this same Carlos Allende, who now signed his name "Carl M. Allen." While the letter was written in the same odd style and bore the same Pennsylvania return address as had the first letter, the stationery carried the letterhead of the Turner Hotel, Gainesville, Texas, and was postmarked Gainesville. (Lest the reader be tempted to write to the Pennsylvania address seeking information, it should be noted that a check with the New Kensington, Pennsylvania, post office in December 1975 revealed that there is no longer any such address either in New Kensington proper or in any of the several RFD routes served by that office. Letters sent to this address would be routinely returned to sender.)

This letter is sometimes erroneously referred to in other sources as the first Allende letter to Dr. Jessup. As we have seen, it is actually the second. The letter is reprinted here, along with a third letter, by courtesy of Dr. Reilly H. Crabb, director of the Borderland Sciences Research Foundation, Inc., Vista, California, who first published them as part of a limited-edition pamphlet in 1962.

> Carlos Miguel Allenda
> R.D. No. 1 Box 223
> New Kensington, Penn.

My Dear Dr. Jessup,

Your invocation to the Public that they move en Masse upon their Representatives and have thusly enough Pressure placed at the right & sufficient Number of Places where from a Law demanding Research into Dr. Albert Einsteins Unified Field Theory May be enacted (1925-27) <u>is Not</u> at all necessary. It May Interest you to know that The Good Doctor Was Not so Much influenced in his retraction of that Work, <u>by</u> Mathematics, as he most assuredly was by Humantics.

His Later computations, done strictly for his own edification & amusement, upon cycles of Human Civilization & Progress compared to the Growth of Mans General overall Character Was enough to Horrify Him. Thus, We are "<u>told</u>" today that that Theory was "Incomplete."

Dr. B. Russell asserts privately that It is complete. He also says that Man is Not Ready for it & Shan't be until after W.W. III. Nevertheless, "Results" of My friend Dr. Franklin Reno, <u>Were used</u>. These Were a complete Recheck of That Theory, With a View to any & Every Possible quick use of it, if feasable in a Very short time. There Were good Results, as far as a Group Math Re-Check AND as far as a good Physical "Result", to Boot. YET, THE NAVY FEARS TO USE THIS RESULT. The Result was and stands today as Proof that The Unified Field Theory to a certain extent is correct. Beyond that certain extent No Person in his right senses, or having any senses at all, Will evermore <u>dare</u> to go. I am sorry that I Mislead You in My Previous Missive. True, enough, such a form of Levitation has been accomplished as described. It is also a Very commonly observed reaction of certain Metals to Certain Fields surrounding a current, This field being used for that purpose. Had Farraday concerned himself about the mag. field surrounding an

Electric Current, We today Would NOT exist
<u>or if</u> We did exist, our present Geo-political
situation would not have the very time-bomb-
ish, ticking off towards Destruction, atmosphere that Now exists. Alright, Alright! The
"result" was complete invisibility of a ship,
Destroyer type, <u>and all</u> of its crew, While at
Sea (Oct. 1943) The Field Was effective in an
oblate spheroidal shape, extending one
hundred yards (More or Less, due to Lunar
position & Latitude) <u>out</u> from each beam of
the ship. Any Person Within <u>that</u> sphere became vague in form BUT He too observed
those Persons aboard that ship as though
they too were of the same state, yet were
walking upon nothing. Any person without
that sphere could see Nothing save the clearly
<u>Defined shape of the Ships Hull in the Water</u>,
PROVIDING of course, that the person was
just close enough to see yet, just barely outside of that field. Why tell you Now? Very
Simple; If You choose to go Mad then you
would reveal this information. Half of the
officers & the crew of that Ship are at Present, Mad as Hatters. A few, are even Yet con-
fined to certain areas where they May receive
trained Scientific aid when they, either, "Go
Blank" or "Go Blank" & Get Stuck." Going-
Blank IS Not at all an unpleasant expierence
to Healthily Curious Sailors. However it is
when also, they "Get Stuck" that they call it

"HELL" INCORPORATED" The Man thusly stricken can Not Move of his own volition unless two or More of those who are within the field go & touch him, quickly, else he "Freezes".

If a man Freezes, His position Must be Marked out carefully and then the Field is cut-off. Everyone but that "Frozen" Man is able to Move; to appreciate <u>apparent</u> Solidity again. Then, the Newest Member of the crew Must approach the Spot, where he will find the "Frozen" Mans face or Bare skin, that is Not covered by usual uniform Clothing. Sometimes, It takes only an hour or so Sometimes all Night & all DayLong & Worse <u>It once took 6 months</u>, to get The man "Unfrozen". <u>This "Deep Freeze" was not psycological</u>. It is the Result of a Hyper-Field that is set up, within the field of the Body, While The "Scorch" Field is turned on & this at Length <u>or</u> upon a Old Hand.

A Highly complicated Piece of Equipment Had to be constructed in order to Unfreeze those who became "True Froze" or "Deep Freeze" subjects. <u>Usually a "Deep Freeze" Man goes Mad, Stark Raving, Gibbering, Running MAD</u>, if His "freeze" is far More than a Day in our time.

"I speak of TIME for DEEP "Frozen Men" are Not aware of Time as We know it. They are Like Semi-comatose person, who Live, breathe, Look & feel but still are unaware of So Utterly Many things as to constitute a "Nether World" to them. A Man in an ordinary common Freeze is aware of Time, Sometimes <u>acutely</u> so. Yet They are <u>Never</u> aware of Time precisely as you or I are aware of it. The First "Deep Freeze" As I said took 6 months to Rectify. It also took over 5 Million Dollars worth of Electronic equipment & a Special Ship Berth. If around or Near the Philadelphia Navy Yard you see a group of Sailors in the act of Putting their Hands <u>upon</u> a fellor <u>or</u> upon "thin air", observe the Digits & appendages of the Stricken Man. If they seem to Waver, as tho within a Heat-Mirage, <u>go quickly</u> & Put YOUR Hands upon Him, <u>For that Man is The Very most Desperate of Men in The World. Not one of those Men ever want at all to become again invisible</u>. I do Not think that Much More Need be said as to Why Man is Not Ready for Force-Field Work. Eh?

You Will Hear phrases from these Men such as "Caught in the Flow (or the Push)" or "Stuck in the Green" or "Stuck in Molasses" or "I was "going" FAST", These Refer to Some of the Decade-later after effects of Force-Field Work. "Caught in the Flow" Describes exactly the "Stuck in Molasses" sensation of a Man going into a "Deep Freeze" or "Plain Freeze" either of the two. "Caught in the

Push" can either refer to That Which a Man feels Briefly WHEN he is either about to inadvertantly "Go-Blank" IE Become Invisible" or about to "Get Stuck" in a "Deep Freeze" or "Plain Freeze."

There are only a very few of the original Expierimental D-E's Crew Left by Now, Sir. Most went insane, one just walked "throo" His quarters Wall in sight of His Wife & Child & 2 other crew Members (WAS NEVER SEEN AGAIN), two "Went into "The Flame," I.E. They "Froze" & caught fire, while carrying common Small-Boat Compasses, one Man carried the compass & Caught fire, the other came for the "Laying on of Hands" as he was the nearest but he too, took fire. THEY BURNED FOR 18 DAYS. The faith in "Hand Laying" Died When this Happened & Mens Minds Went by the scores. The expieriment Was a Complete Success. The Men were Complete Failures.

Check Philadelphia Papers for a tiny one Paragraph (upper Half of sheet, inside the paper Near the rear 3rd of Paper, 1944-46 in Spring or Fall or Winter, NOT Summer.) of an Item describing the Sailors Actions after their initial Voyage. They Raided a Local to the Navy Yard "Gin Mill" or "Beer Joint" & caused such Shock & Paralysis of the Waitresses that Little comprehensible could be gotten from them, save that Paragraph & the Writer of it, Does Not Believe it, & Says "I only wrote what I heard & them Dames is Daffy. So, all I get is a "Hide-it" Bedtime Story."

Check observer ships crew, Matson Lines Liberty ship out of Norfolk, (Company MAY Have Ships Log for that Voyage or Coast Guard have it) The S.S. Andrew Furuseth, Chief Mate Mowsely, (Will secure Captains Name Later) (Ships Log Has Crew List on it.) one crew member Richard Price or "Splicey" Price May Remember other Names of Deck Crew Men, (Coast Guard has record of Sailors issued "Papers") Mr. Price Was 18 or 19 then, Oct. 1943, and Lives or Lived at that time in His old Family Home in Roanoke, V.A. a small town with a Small phone book. These Men Were Witnesses, The Men of this crew, "Connally of New England, (Boston?), May have Witnessed but I doubt it. (Spelling May be incorrect) DID Witness this. I ask you to Do this bit of Research simply that you May Choke on your own Tongue when you Remember what you have "appealed be Made Law"

> Very Disrespectfully Yours,
>
> Carl M. Allen

P.S. Will Help More if you see Where I can. (Z416175)

Days Later

Notes in addition to and pertaining to Missive. (Contact Rear Admiral Rawson Bennett for verification of info Herein. Navy Chief of Research. He may offer you a job, ultimately.)

Coldly and analytically speaking, without the Howling that is in the Letter to you accompanying this, I will say the following in all Fairness to you & to Science. (1) The Navy did Not know that the men could become invisible WHILE NOT UPON THE SHIP & UNDER THE FIELDS INFLUENCE. (2) The Navy Did Not know that <u>there would be</u> Men Die from odd effects of HYPER "Field" within or upon "Field". (3) Further, They even yet do Not know Why this happened & are not even sure that the "F" within "F" is the reason, for sure at all. <u>In Short</u> The Atomic bomb didn't kill the expierimentors thus the expieriments went on—but eventually one or two were accidentally killed But <u>the cause</u> was known as to Why they died. Myself, I "feel" that something pertaining to that Small-boat compass "triggered" off "The Flames." I have no proof, but Neither Does the Navy. (4) WORSE & Not Mentioned When one or two of their Men, Visible-within-the-field-to-all-the-others, <u>Just Walked into Nothingness</u>, AND Nothing Could be felt, of them, either when the "field" Was turned on OR off, THEY WERE JUST GONE! <u>Then</u>, More Fears Were Amassed. (5) Worse, Yet, When an apparently Visible & New-Man Just walks seemingly "throo" the Wall of his House, the surrounding area Searched by all Men & thoroughly scrutinized by & with & under an Installed Protable Field developer AND NOTHING EVER found of him. <u>So Many Many Fears were by then in effect that the Sum total of them all could Not ever again be faced by ANY of those Men or by the Men Working at & upon the Experiments</u>.

I wish to Mention that Somehow, also, The Experimental Ship Disappeared from its Philadelphia Dock and only a Very few Minutes Later appeared at its other Dock in the Norfolk, Newport News, Portsmouth area. This was distinctly AND clearly Identified as being that place BUT the ship then, <u>again</u>, Disappeared And Went <u>Back</u> to its Philadelphia Dock in only a Very few Minutes or Less. This was also noted in the newspapers But I forget what paper I read it in or When It happened. Probably Late in the experiments, May have been in 1946 <u>after</u> Experiments were discontinued, I can Not Say for Sure.

To the Navy this Whole thing was So Impractical due to its Morale Blasting effects Which were so much so that efficient operation of the Ship was Drastically hindered and then after this occurrence It was shown that even the Mere operation of a ship could Not be counted upon at all. In short, Ignorance of this thing bred Such Terrors of it that, on the Level of attempted operations, with what knowledge was then available It was deemed as impossible, Impracticable and Too Horrible.

I believe that Had YOU then been Working upon & With the team that was Working upon this project With yourself knowing what You NOW know, that "The Flames" Would Not have been so unexpected, or Such a Terrifying Mystery. Also, More than Likely, I must say in All fairness, None of these other occurrences could have happened without some knowledge of their possibility of occuring. In fact, They May have been prevented by a far More Cautious Program AND by a Much more Cautiously careful Selection of Personnell for Ships officers & Crew. Such was not the case. The Navy used whatever Human Material was at hand, Without Much, if any, thought as to character & Personality of that Material. If care, Great Care is taken in selection of Ship, and officers and crew AND If Careful Indoctrination is taken along with Careful watch over articles of apparel Such as rings & Watches & Identification bracelets & belt buckles, Plus AND ESPECIALLY the effect of Hob-Nailed shoes or Cleated-shoes U.S. Navy issue shoes, I feel that some progress towards dissipating the fearfilled ignorance surrounding this project Will be Most surely & certainly accomplished. The Records of the U.S. Maritime <u>Service</u> HOUSE Norfolk, Va (for Graduated Seamen of their Schools) Will reveal Who was assigned to S.S. Andrew Furuseth for Month of either Late Sept. or Oct. of 1943. I remember positively of one other observer who stood beside Me When tests were going on. He was from New England, Brown Blond Curly Hair, blue eyes, Don't remember Name. I leave it up <u>to you</u> to Decide if further Work shall be put into this or Not, and Write this in Hopes there will be.

Very Sincerely,

Carl M. Allen

Invisible ships? Disappearing crew members?? A wild and fantastic tale indeed—but surely an intriguing one as well to a man of Jessup's interests. According to Vincent Gaddis' brief account of the affair, published as part of his book *Invisible Horizons* in 1964: "Jessup's first reaction was that the letter was either a hoax or the rantings of a crackpot. The very nature of UFO investigation attracts twisted and unstable minds."

But, Gaddis continued, Jessup still felt there was a possibility that "the writer was giving an exaggerated account of an actual occurrence.

There were many classified experiments made during World War II. In 1943, research was in progress that led to the creation of the atomic bomb. It had been inspired by Einstein's letter to President Roosevelt. The 'Unified Field' theory of this famed scientist could also have been the basis for other, not so successful experimentation."

If indeed the letter was a fabrication of some sort, then why the inclusion of so much detail with regard to names, places, and events? It is hardly usual for a hoaxer to go out of his way to provide his intended victim with the sort of details that might result in exposure of his hoax. Jessup was perplexed.

Finally, moved by an inexplicable sense of urgency and by the same curiosity that had motivated him the first time, Jessup answered the letter—this time by postcard on which he noted that he considered it of "the greatest importance" that Allende send him "at once" evidence of any sort which would serve to support the strange allegations he had made.

As before, months passed without reply. Jessup, still busy with other matters, assumed the incident had finally been laid to rest, and after the first few weeks, he seldom thought about it.

Nearly five months later, however, Pandora's box opened again to disgorge yet another Allende missive—this one every bit as cryptic as the other two. The postmark read "DuBois,

Pennsylvania, May 25, 1956," and the text
(again courtesy of Dr. Crabb) read as follows:

Carlos M. Allende
RF 1 Box 223
New Kensington, Pa.

Dear Mr. Jessup:

Having just recently gotten home from my
long travels around the country I find that
you had dropped me a card. You ask that I
write you "at once" and So after taking everything into consideration, I have decided to do
so. You ask me for what is tantamount to
positive proof of something that only the du-
plication of those devices that produced "This
phenomenon" could ever give you. at least,
were I of scientific bent, I presume that, were
I of Such a Curiosity about something, the
which has been produced from a theory that
was discarded (1927) as incomplete, I am sure
that I would be of such a dubiousness that I
would Have to be <u>shown</u> those devices that
produced such a curious interaction of Forces
& Fields, in operation & their product Mr.
Jessup, I could NEVER possibly satisfy such
an attitude. The reason being that I could
not, Nor ever would the Navy Research Dept.
(Then under the present boss of the Navy,
Burke) ever let it be known that any such
thing was ever allowed to be done. For you
see, It was because of Burke's Curiosity &

Willingness & prompting that this experiment was enabled to be carried out. It proved a White-elephant <u>but</u> His attitude towards advanced & ultra-advanced types of research is just "<u>THE</u>" THING that put him where he is today. (Or at least, to be sure, It carries a great weight). Were the stench of such an Experiments results EVER to come out, He would be crucified.

However, I have noticed, that throo the ages, those who have had this happen to them, once the vulgar passions that caused the reaction have colled-off AND <u>further</u> research OPENLY carried on, <u>that</u> these crucified ones achieve something akin to Saint hood. You say that this, "is of the greatest importance". I disagree with you Mr. Jessup, not just whole Heartedly, <u>but vehemently</u>. However at the same time, your ideas & your own sort of curiosity is that of mine own sort and besides my disagreement is based upon philosophical Morality and not upon that curiosity which Drives Science so rapidly. I can be of some positive help to you in myself but to do so would require a Hypnotist, Sodium Pentathol, a tape recorder & an excellent typist-secretary in order to produce material of <u>Real</u> value to you.

As you know one who is hypnotized cannot Lie and one who is both hypnotized AND given "Truth serum" as it is colloqually known COULD NOT POSSIBLY LIE, <u>AT</u>

<u>ALL</u>. To boot, <u>My Memory</u> would be THUS enabled to remember things in such <u>great detail,</u> things that my present consciousness cannot recall at all, or only barely and uncertainly that it would be of far greater benifit to use hypnosis. I could thus be enabled to <u>not only</u> Recall COMPLETE Names, but also addresses & telephone numbers AND perhaps the <u>very important</u> Z numbers of those sailors whom I sailed with them or even came into contact with. I could too, being something of a Dialectician, be able to thusly talk exactly as these witnesses talked and imitate or <u>illustrate</u> their Mannerisms & <u>Habits of thought,</u> thus your psychologists can figure IN ADVANCE the Surefire method of dealing Most Successfully with these. I could NOT do this with someone with whom I had not observed at length & these men, I lived with for about 6 months, so you are bound to get good to excellent results. <u>The mind does NOT ever forget, Not really, As you know.</u> Upon this I suggest this way of doing this with Myself but further, the Latter usage of Myself in Mannerism & Thought pattern illustration is suggested in order that the Goal of inducing these Men <u>to place themselves</u> at & under your disposal (HYPNOTICALLY OR UNDER TRUTH SERUM) is a Goal, the Which could Have Far greater impact, due to co-relation of Expieriences remembered Hypnotically <u>by Men who have</u>

NOT seen or even written to each other, at all, for Nearly or over TEN years. In this, With such Men as Witnesses, giving irreffutable testimony It is my belief that were Not the Navy, but the Airforce, confronted with such evidence, (IE Chief of Research) there would be either an uproar or a quiet and determined effort to achieve SAFELY "that which" the Navy failed at. They did NOT fail to, I hope you realize, achieve Metalic & organic invisibility nor did they fail to, unbesoughtedly, achieve transportaton of thousands of tons of Metal & Humans at an eyes blink speed. Even though this latter effect of prolonged experimentation was. (to them) The thing that caused them to consider the experiment as a failure, I BELIEVE THAT FURTHER EXPERIMENTS WOULD NATURALLY HAVE PRODUCED CONTROLLED TRANSPORT OF GREAT TONNAGES AT ULTRA-FAST SPEEDS TO A DESIRED POINT THE INSTANT IT IS DESIRED throo usage of an area covered by: (1) those cargoes and (2) that "Field" that could cause those goods, Ships or Ship parts (MEN WERE TRANSPORTED AS WELL) to go to another Point. Accidentally & to the embarressed perplexity of the Navy THIS HAS ALREADY HAPPENED TO A WHOLE SHIP, CREW & ALL. I read of this AND of THE OFF-BASE AWOL ACTIVITIES OF THE crew-Men who were at the time invisible in a Philadelphia NEWSPAPER. UNDER NARCO-HYPNOSIS I CAN BE ENABLED TO DIVULGE THE NAME, DATE & SECTION & PAGE NUMBER of that Paper & the other one. Thus this papers "Morgue" will divulge EVEN MORE POSITIVE PROOF ALREADY PUBLISHED of this experiment. The Name of the REPORTER who skeptically covered & wrote of these incidents (OF THE RESTAURANT-BARROOM RAID WHILE INVISIBLE & OF THE SHIPS SUDDEN AWOL) AND WHO INTERVIEWED the Waitresses CAN THUS BE FOUND, thus HIS and the Waitresses testimony can be added to the Records. Once on this track, I believe That you can uncover CONSIDERABLY MORE evidence to sustain this———(what would you call it——SCANDAL or DISCOVERY?) You would Need a Dale Carneigie to Maneuver these folks into doing just as you wish. It would be cheaper than paying everyone of all these witnesses & Much more Ethical. The Idea Is, to the Layman type of person, utterly ridiculous. However, can you remember, all by yourself, the Date of a Newspaper in which you saw an interesting item more than 5 years ago? Or recall names of Men, their phone #s that you saw in 1943-44.

I do hope you will consider this plan. You will Progress as Not possible in any other way. Of course, I realize that you would need a Man Who can cause people to want to have fun, to play with Hypnotism, one that can thusly those he-you need to: #1 come to His Demonstration & thus call on them to be either or both "Honored" as Helping with the show" & for doing Him a Great favor, &/or being part of the act for the mite of a small fee He would HAVE to be a Man of such an adroit ingenuity at Manufacturing a plausable story on the-instant-he-sizes-up-his-" personality-to be dealt with THAT had cost PLENTY. The ability to convince people of an outright Lie as being the absolute truth would be one of his prime prerequisites. (Ahem.) Yes, some such skulduggery would have to be thought well out & done. THE ULTIMATE END WILL BE A TRUTH TOO HUGE, TOO FANTASTIC, TO NOT BE TOLD. A WELL FOUNDED TRUTH, BACKED UP BY UNOBFUSCATIVE PROOF POSITIVE. I would like to find where it is that these Sailors live NOW. IT is known that some few people can somehow tell you a mans name & His Home address UNDER HYPNOSIS EVEN THOUGH NEVER HAVING EVER MET OR SEEN THE PERSON. These folks have a very high or just a high PSI factor in their make-up that can be intensified under stress or strain OR that usually is intensified under extreme fright. It also can be Re-intensified by Hypnosis, thus is like reading from the Encyclopedia Britanica. Even though that Barroom-Restaurant Raid was staged by invisible or partly invisible men, those men <u>CAN SEE EACH OTHER THUS</u> NAMES, In the excitement, were sure to have been Mentioned, whether last or first Names or Nicknames. A check of the Naval Yards Dispensories or Hospital of aid stations or prison RECORDS of that particular day that the Barroom-Restaurant occured May reveal the EXACT NAMES OF PRECISELY WHO WERE THE MEN, THEIR SERVICE SERIAL NUMBERS & THUS THE INFORMATION ON WHERE THEY ARE <u>FROM</u> BE SECURED & by adroit "Maneuvuerings" of those still at Home, <u>THE NAME</u> OF THE PLACE where they are at present can be secured.

HOW WOULD YOU LIKE TO ACTUALLY SPEAK TO (or some of <u>THE MEN</u>) A MAN WHO WAS ONCE <u>AN INVISIBLE HUMAN BEING</u>? (MAY BECOME SO IN FRONT OF YOUR VERY EYES IF HE TURNS-OFF HIS HIP SET) Well, all this fantastically Preposterous sort of rubbish <u>will be</u> necessary, Just to do that, the Hypnotist-psychologist & all that. Maybe I suggest something <u>too</u> thorough & <u>too</u> Methodical for your taste but then, I, as first subject, Don't care to be Hypnotized <u>at all</u>, But too, feel that certain pull of curiosity about this thing that, to me, is irresistable. I want to crack this thing wide open. My reasons are simply to enable more work to be done upon this "Field Theory."

I am a star-gazer Mr. Jessup. I make no bones about this and the fact that I feel that IF HANDLED PROPERLY, I.E. PRE- SENTED TO PEOPLE & SCIENCE IN THE PROPER PSYCHOLOGICALLY EFFEC- TIVE MANNER, I feel sure that Man will go where He now dreams of being—to the stars via the form of transport that the Navy ac- cidentally stumbled upon (to their embar- rassment) when their EXP. SHIP took off & popped-up a minute or so later on several Hundred sea travel-trip miles away at an- other of its Berths in the Chesapeake Bay area. I read of this in another news paper & only by Hypnosis could any Man remember all the details of which paper, date of occur- ance & etc., you see? Eh. Perhaps already, the Navy has used this accident of transport to build your UFO's. It is a logical advance from any standpoint. What do you think???

VERY RESPECTFULLY

Carl Allen

Hypnosis? Truth serum? UFO propulsion sys- tems? It is certainly not too difficult to imagine the thoughts which must have raced through Jessup's mind after reading this one. Had he somehow stumbled onto one of the biggest stories of the decade, or was he being set up as the patsy for one of its most elaborate hoaxes?

But if Jessup had been perplexed up to this point, it was nothing compared to what was soon to follow. For as he pondered what his reaction should be to this latest development, even stranger events were beginning to unfold elsewhere.

CHAPTER 3

The Navy
Takes Note

Had the story ended here, it seems almost certain that Dr. Jessup would have been more than happy to write off the entire matter of these strange letters as the ravings of a crackpot. Several people who knew him agree that in spite of his earlier interest in the matter, he had finally arrived at the very comfortable conclusion that the letters were too fantastic to put much stock in.

Although it is not known whether Jessup ever bothered to answer the third letter or not, it seems safe to assume that if he eventually did it was probably just to hedge his bet. But whether he answered or not is in itself relatively unimportant to what follows. What is known is that Jessup was much too busy trying to drum up support for another expedition to Mexico to run down fantastic stories about disappearing ships and invisible crews. His immediate goal was obviously to get another look at those craters.

It was, in fact, with this objective in mind that he wrote the following to Gray Barker, one of his less mysterious correspondents, late in 1956:

> Of course, you know of my interests in Mexico, and they have suddenly and unexpectedly come to life: (1) Some commercial interests are probably taking me to Mexico on a preliminary survey for minerals under the meteor craters; and (2) it seems very likely that the government may finance an expedition through the sponsorship of the Univ. of Michigan. On the first, I would leave, probably about Dec. 10, for a five-week trip. On the second, it might materialize about April 1 (1957) and last for at least five months.... as [yet] no contracts have been signed.

Although, unfortunately, both of these "opportunities" later fell through, Jessup was at this point in an exultant state of mind, and a high degree of expectation and anticipation is evident in his letters. Coupling this with the fact that he was working on what he considered to be another major book, (*The Expanding Case for the UFO*), it is not hard to understand why he would be tempted to postpone consideration of less pressing matters, and among these would certainly have been the Allende letters. Perhaps when he had more time and wanted something to do he would look into them—but for now, they would keep.

However, in spite of Jessup's confident belief that the letters were a dead issue, things that he had no immediate way of knowing about or controlling were beginning to take place—a series of extremely curious coincidences.

It should be noted here in all fairness that there are several accounts of the story that follows—all differing from one another to a greater or lesser degree depending upon how far from the original sources they managed to stray before being written down by an interested party. Having taken all of this into account, we have attempted to reconstruct the version that follows from what appear to be the most reliable of the sources of information. In so doing, first-hand accounts from those who knew Jessup personally have been given greater weight over versions which are obviously secondhand or thirdhand.

This part of the story appears to have had its beginnings in late July or early August 1955—which, if this date is accurate, is at least several months *before* Jessup received the first of his series of perplexing letters from Allende. In any event, it all began with a manila envelope addressed to "Admiral N. Furth, Chief, Office of Naval Research, Washington 25, D.C.," which, we are told, was included in the incoming correspondence of one Major Darrell L. Ritter, USMC Aeronautical Project Officer at ONR (Office of Naval Research). This envelope was postmarked "Seminole, Texas, 1955" and across the face of it had been scrawled the words

"Happy Easter" in ink. Inside, without return address or letter of explanation, was a paperback copy of Morris Jessup's *The Case for the UFO.* Upon opening the book, Ritter saw that it had been heavily marked up with handwritten annotations and underlinings of a most perplexing sort written in at least three different colors of ink—annotations which seemed to imply that the writer of them possessed intimate knowledge of UFOs, their means of propulsion, origin, background, and history. The book itself was well worn, and whoever was responsible for this work had apparently spent a great amount of time doing it.

Admiral Furth himself does not appear to have been interested in such unsigned rubbish—if indeed he was ever shown the book at all—but Major Ritter seems to have regarded it as something of an interesting curiosity. At least it appears to have been thanks to him that the book was not instantly thrown away. Ritter most likely kept the book himself when he saw that Furth wasn't interested, and must have spent much of his spare time going through it. His immediate reactions to what he found are not recorded, but reading the book along with its collection of bizarre annotations must have left him in a state of wonderment. The annotations seemed to be explanations of the mysterious disappearances of ships, planes, and people, discussed in Jessup's books, many of them within the area of the mysterious "Bermuda Triangle." Further, they elaborated,

Meeting of the Project Orbiter Committee (the group that contacted Dr. Jessup) on March 17, 1955, in Washington, D.C. Seated, left to right: Cdr. George W. Hoover, Office of Naval Research; Frederick C. Durant III, Arthur D. Little, Inc.; James B. Kendrick, Aerophysics Development Corp.; William A. Giardini, Alabama Tool and Die; Philippe W. Newton, Department of Defense; Rudolf H. Schlidt, Army Ballistic Missile Agency; Gerhard Heller, ABMA; Wernher von Braun; ABMA. Standing: Lt. Cdr. William E. Dowdell, USN; Alexander Satin, ONR; Cdr. Robert C. Truax, UDN; Liston Tatum, IBM; Austin W. Stanton, Varo, Inc.; Fred L. Whipple, Harvard University; George W. Petri, IBM; Lowell O. Anderson, ONR; Milton W. Rosen, NRL (Smithsonian Institution)

sometimes in considerable detail, upon the origin of the many "odd storms and clouds, objects falling from the sky, strange marks and footprints, and other matters" which Jessup had written about. Mentioned also was the construction of undersea cities in connection with two groups of presumably extraterrestrial creatures referred to as "the L-M's" and "the S-M's," only one of which (the "L-M's") was to be regarded as friendly. In addition, odd terms—mothership, home ship, dead ship, great ark, great bombardment, great return, great war, littlemen, force fields, deep freeze, measure markers, scout ships, magnetic fields, gravity fields, sheets of diamond, cosmic rays, force cutters, inlay work, clear talk, telepathing, nodes, vortices, magnetic net—were found throughout the various handwritten annotations.

It is quite possible that Major Ritter, who knew of the emphasis being placed on antigravity research by the military at the time, felt that perhaps he had stumbled upon some sort of a clue to the matter. But whatever his motives, we can be certain that it was he who preserved the book because it was from his hands that Commander George W. Hoover, ONR's Special Projects Officer, together with Captain Sidney Sherby, a newcomer to the ONR, received the book a few months later, after they had expressed an interest in it. Both of these men were deeply involved in the Navy's then current Project Vanguard, the code name for America's efforts to develop its first earth satellite and were interested in antigravity research as well.

Commander Hoover was evidently so much intrigued by the weird scribblings and strange marginal notations that he was willing to devote significant amounts of his personal time to a pursuit of the matter in an attempt to determine exactly what, if anything, was behind it all. Captain Sherby was interested too, and they spent considerable time discussing the strangeness of the matter. It was in this way that sometime in the spring of 1957 Morris Jessup received a letter from either Sherby or Hoover inviting him to visit the Office of Naval Research in Washington to discuss his book.

When he arrived, Jessup was handed the same marked-up paperback copy of *The Case for the UFO* which had fallen into Major Ritter's hands some eighteen months earlier.

"This book was sent to us through the mail anonymously," one of the officers explained. "Apparently it was passed back and forth among at least three persons who made notations." (An erroneous assumption based upon the use of three colors of ink and the impression several of the annotations gave of being a conversation directed from one person to another. In actuality, there appears to have actually been only one annotator.) "Look it over, Mr. Jessup, and tell us if you have any idea who wrote those comments."

According to Vincent Gaddis' account, "As Morris Jessup went through this annotated copy he became increasingly alarmed because ever more of the comments appeared to concern matters of which he had heard but which were not mentioned in his book. Further, the person or persons who wrote these marginal notes and comments obviously knew a great deal about the then current "folklore" of UFOs, extraterrestrials, and many other related matters usually of concern mainly to psychics, cultists, and mystics. That these were true or not was not the point. The fact that they should be so precisely known to an unknown was.

Jessup was troubled. Why, he wondered, was the Navy interested in something so obviously the product of a deranged mind? But as to who could possibly have produced such a thing, he couldn't imagine—couldn't, that is, until he happened to notice a certain curious passage which made pointed reference to a secret naval experiment which allegedly occurred in 1943. Realizing that he had encountered such a statement before, Jessup continued to turn pages. Upon finding a few more direct references to the disappearing ship, he was left without a doubt—his erstwhile mysterious correspondent, Carlos Miguel Allende, had to be connected in some way with this strange book. Satisfied with his conclusions, Jessup at this point is reported to have looked up and commented that he felt certain that he had at least two letters in his files "from one of the commentators."

"Thank you, Mr. Jessup," Hoover replied. "It is important that we see those letters." Hoover then went on to inform Jessup that he was interested in all of this to such an extent that he had already taken the liberty of arranging for Jessup's book to be reproduced complete with all the mysterious annotations in a "limited edition for circulation among some of our top people." And he promised, "We'll see that you get a copy."

Jessup must have complied with Hoover's request, since the letters were later reproduced as a part of the "introduction" to the special "limited edition" of Jessup's book that Hoover had arranged for. (Hoover and Sherby apparently wrote the rest of the introduction.)

A source close to Jessup even goes so far as to state that Jessup made a total of three separate visits to ONR about the matter.

The task of reproducing this book by the slow and laborious process of retyping it in its entirety complete with annotations on mimeograph stencils (these were pre-Xerox days) and then running off copies in two colors (black for the text and red for the annotations and underlinings) on standard 8½ x 11 paper was undertaken by the Varo Manufacturing Company of Garland, Texas—a "space-age" firm heavily involved in military research contracts and one with which Hoover and Sherby are known to have had significant connections, since both were later to find employment with the firm. Whether the cost of the project was assumed by Varo, the Office of Naval Research, or Sherby and Hoover personally, remains unclear. What is known is that the typing was done by a Miss Michael (Michelle?) Ann Dunn, personal secretary to the then president of Varo, Austin N. Stanton, and that the mimeograph machine belonged to a division of that company known as "Military Assistance."

One source maintains that Miss Dunn was not in fact Mr. Stanton's secretary, but only a temporary employee hired especially for this one job. Indeed, Varo itself denies any record of a "Miss Dunn" ever having been employed by the firm.

Exactly 127 copies were produced (other sources have given the number as anywhere between 12 and 25), complete with Hoover and Sherby's already mentioned unsigned three-page introduction and appendices containing typed copies of the two letters Jessup had received from Carlos Miguel Allende. The printed pages were laboriously collated by hand and spiral-bound between pale-blue cardboard covers.

In retrospect, it appears that Sherby and Hoover's interest in this book stemmed from their belief, as set forth in the introduction, that "because of the importance we attach to the possibility of discovering clues to the nature of gravity, no possible item, however disreputable from the point of view of classical science, should be overlooked." Exactly what "clues to the nature of gravity" were being referred to is not exactly clear, however, since there appear to be only a few (although admittedly rather tantalizing) references to this matter in the annotations of the Varo edition itself outside of Jessup's own vague comments concerning it.

Nonetheless, for whatever obscure reasons, there can be very little doubt that the resultant "book" was indeed circulated for a time in Washington military circles. On this aspect of the matter, UFO researcher and publisher Gray Barker, long one of the prime movers in trying to solve the mystery of the Allende letters, commented in his 1963 book *The Strange Case of Dr. M.K. Jessup* as follows:

I first learned of the annotated copy when I was talking to Mrs. Walton Colcord John, director of the Little Listening Post, a UFO and New Age Publication in Washington. Speaking over the telephone, Mrs. John told me of a strange rumor going around, to the effect that somebody had sent a marked-up copy to Washington and that the government had gone to the expense of mimeographing the entire book, so that all the underlinings and notations could be added to the original text. This was being sent around rather widely, she told me, through military channels.

She had not, of course, seen a copy of it, and didn't know too much about it, but somehow seemed to connect it with an alleged Naval experiment wherein a ship had completely disappeared from sight. I couldn't make too much out of all this until later I

had also heard about the strange Allende
Letters, which told of such an experiment in
a most horrifying way.

But, since it is Jessup and the mystifying
Allende letters themselves rather than the
Varo annotated edition of *The Case for the UFO*
that constitute our main thread of interest in
this study, we must not digress further at this
point but continue with our investigation.
(Should the reader wish to pursue the matter
of the annotated book any further, reprint fac-
similes of the original Varo edition may be obtained through Mr. Barker at Saucerian Press,
P.O. Box 2228, Clarksburg, West Virginia
26302.)

Just exactly what effect all these unexpected
developments had on Dr. Jessup is difficult to
determine completely, but it appears that coupled with a car accident and marital difficulties,
experienced by him at that time, they consti-
tuted a shock from which he was never able to
recover fully. Again relying on the personal accounts of those closest to Jessup, one thing that
seems certain is that after Jessup received his
promised copies (three) of the Varo reprint from
ONR, he spent a great deal of time going over
the book in detail. Reportedly he was so disturbed at the truly bizarre contents of these
annotations that he took the trouble to "rean-
notate" the book by typing his own comments
and reactions on slips of paper and sticking
them in approximately every tenth page or so.

(This reannotated copy is apparently still in existence, but has not been made generally available to researchers by its owner.)

Meanwhile, the extent of Sherby and Hoover's interest in the affair is further confirmed by the fact that one (or perhaps both) of them had apparently been making efforts to locate Carlos Allende.

Reportedly a trip by Hoover to the rural Pennsylvania address given by Allende in his letters to Jessup proved fruitless—as did all attempts to locate him by other traditional methods. Allende, it seemed, had disappeared. In addition to the Navy men's efforts, an unnamed friend of Dr. Jessup's is also said to have tried to locate Allende at this same address (perhaps at Jessup's request?) with the same results. According to this report, the man found the farmhouse vacant and succeeded only in learning from neighbors that a man named Carlos or Carl had roomed there for some time with an elderly couple and then had moved on. Sometime after that, a truck had pulled up to the house, the elderly couple and their belongings were loaded up, and the truck was driven off—destination unknown.

Jessup, a trained astrophysicist, found it difficult to imagine why the Navy was going to all this trouble unless there was, in fact, something to it all. There seems little doubt that the circumstances of the alleged invisibility experiment were of special interest to him, and it appears that he spent at least some of his time looking into the possibilities.

Jessup, after the collapse of his hopes for exploring the Mexican craters, had by 1958, it seems, all but given up his professorial duties in an attempt to make a living through writing and publishing. Although not immediately successful in this pursuit, he apparently felt free enough to continue trying for a while even if it meant living on a somewhat reduced income, since his children were all grown and had moved away and his wife had left him. Accordingly, after seeing to it that the large house he owned outside of Miami was closed, he moved back to his native Indiana, where he set himself up as editor of a small astrological publication. Here he continued to try to pursue his writing career while at the same time becoming more and more interested in psychic phenomena—perhaps because he regarded this as one possible way of explaining some of his increasingly troubled personal feelings. Those who kept in touch with him during these months describe him as showing evidence of considerable inner emotional turmoil and as increasingly tense and troubled. In fact, one of his psychic friends who accepted a dinner invitation from him in early 1958 during one of Jessup's visits to Ann Arbor is said to have commented on how shocked she was at "the change in his vibrations." "They had," she rather quaintly observed, "taken on . . . a sort of astral BO."

The beginning of the end came in late October 1958, when Jessup traveled from Indiana to

New York, ostensibly for the purpose of contacting astrological organizations and publishers. Such a trip, on the surface at least, did not appear to be out of the ordinary for him, since he had made many trips to New York in the past and had succeeded in accumulating numerous contacts there. Consequently those who knew him in that city little suspected that it was to be his last visit with them.

On or about Halloween evening, Jessup, in response to a dinner invitation, paid a visit to the home of one of his friends in New York—the prominent naturalist Ivan T. Sanderson. Sanderson had founded the Society for the Investigation of the Unexplained (SITU), now situated at Little Silver, New Jersey. He published an account of Jessup's last visit in Issue No. 4 (September 1968) of his society's journal, *Pursuit*, from which the following is freely quoted:

> Then, in 1958, a whole series of most mysterious events took place.... The most outlandish things then began to happen, which provide ample material for a full-length book in themselves. They ended in a really ghastly tragedy.
>
> On a certain day...Morris Jessup was a guest in my home in New York. There were about a dozen people present, off and on, before, during, and after dinner. At one point Morris asked three of us if we could have a chat in my private office. To this we repaired; and he then handed us the original reanno-

tated copy, and asked us in great sincerity to read it, then lock it up in safekeeping "in case anything should happen to me." This appeared all very dramatic at the time but, after we had read this material, we must admit to having developed a collective feeling of a most unpleasant nature....

Morris was a devoted family man and especially solicitious of the future welfare of his grandchildren. At this our last meeting he was extremely distraught and admitted that, due to an originally pure intellectual interest in natural phenomena, he found that he had been completely swept into a weird and insane world of unreality. He expressed outright terror at the endless stream of "coincidences" that had occurred in his work and in his private life; but, beyond this, he was distressed that he might be accused of outright insanity should he mention these aggravations and related matters.

What he actually said to us was in substance: I don't think I'm going balmy but I do believe all this nonsense is actually happening and is not a figment of my imagination. If you read this book you will see why I have been forced to this conclusion. Now, if I am right, I have a feeling that this just can't go on any longer without something unpleasant happening; and, if something does and anybody reads *this* material, they will immediately say that I obviously went around the bend; and once that has been even suggested, you know quite well that the average uninvolved citizen will immediately jump to the conclusion that there is insanity in my family.

This was a pretty tragic situation on the face of it even then. Naturally we gave our solemn promise that Morris' request would be scrupulously observed; while he, for his part, added the rider that only if certain persons he named requested in writing (and with accompanying legal affidavits) that we do so, should the material be published.

Sanderson went on to state that he had been "repeatedly asked" to reveal the name of the person to whom Jessup chose to give his material for safekeeping that evening, but that he "just as repeatedly refused to do so" and would "continue to do so." So far as is known, he scrupulously kept his word right up to the time of his death in 1973—although certain coincidences have led the authors to suspect that the man whom Jessup chose was none other than Sanderson himself.

Jessup was scheduled to return to his Indiana residence within the next couple of days, so no one was really surprised when he left New York a day or two after Sanderson's dinner party. But when, as the days went by, he failed to show up in Indiana, certain people, his publishers among them, began to fear for his safety. Finally, after about ten days had passed without word, they somehow obtained the name of one of Jessup's business associates in New York and wrote him asking for information concerning Jessup's whereabouts. They were dismayed to learn that the man did not know.

Finally, in mid-December 1958, about a month after Jessup's publisher's concerned letter of inquiry and fully six weeks after his departure from New York, again according to Sanderson, "another of his friends in New York learned that he was in Florida, had gone there directly from New York, had opened his house, and a few days later had been involved in a very serious car accident from which he was still recovering."

Little is known of Jessup's life during the next few months save that his state of morbid despondence and depression increased rather rapidly during that time. This unfortunate situation was aggravated by his accident, which had left him unable to accomplish much he regarded of any value, by his publisher's rejection of several of his manuscripts as "not up to par," and by continued criticism of his writings from various scientific and academic circles around the country. In any event, there seems to be little doubt that he spent a great deal of time planning what he must do with his life from that point.

In mid-April 1959, less than two months after his fifty-ninth birthday, he decided on the final act. In a long "depressing and depressed" letter to his principal confidant in New York, a well-known late-night talk-show host on WOR,

"Long John" Nebel (now deceased), Jessup poured out his soul. The letter, described as a "straight suicide note," made it clear that he now felt himself to be " a complete vegetable," and, after asking that certain wishes be carried out on his behalf, made it clear in no uncertain terms that he preferred to take the risk of "another existence of universe being better than this miserable world." He had, he said, arrived at this solution only after careful consideration and not in any fit of sudden desperation.

His final wish, communicated by him in the letter to Nebel, was that if he did kill himself, Nebel was to arrange for a séance to be conducted on his all-night radio show for the purpose of trying to determine if communication after death was possible. According to Paris Flammonde, the producer of the "Long John Nebel Show" for many years, the program was completely arranged and was about to go on the air when it was "aborted by Mr. Nebel's attorney, who felt that the privacy of certain persons might be violated."

While reliable reports have it that Dr. Jessup wrote at least two other such notes to close friends, the actual number of their contents is relatively unimportant. On April 20, 1959, at about 6:30 P.M., the still barely breathing body of Dr. Morris K. Jessup, noted author, sometime astronomer, and one of the world's first freethinkers on the UFO phenomenon, was discovered slumped over the wheel of his station wagon, which, according to the information on his death certificate, he had parked in rural Dade County Park not far from his Coral Gables home. It is said that he died only moments later, either on the way to the hospital or shortly after having arrived there—a victim of self-inflicted carbon-monoxide poisoning by means of a hose which was attached to the exhaust pipe of the car and passed into the passenger compartment through a nearly closed window. As we shall see later, there were some who suggested it wasn't suicide.

Ivan Sanderson, one of Jessup's closest friends, was moved to comment some years later that it was the consensus of several of Jessup's friends and associates who had once gotten together to discuss the matter that the bizarre events surrounding the "Allende case" were directly responsible for triggering the "chain of events" which ultimately led to Jessup's tragic death. In *Uninvited Visitors,* he described Jessup as "an ebullient enthusiast ... almost too enthusiastic and confident of his theories" prior to receiving the letters. After that, "he seemed to suddenly doubt everything." Sanderson went on:

"He told us in his last meeting that he frankly just could not 'think cosmically,' explaining that the concepts put forward by Allende in his letters and the annotations in the book were beyond his comprehension but set at naught all he thought he had gained in knowledge of what he had always considered was a fairly straightforward and more or less 'insulated' business—namely, the UFOs."

While Sanderson pictured Jessup as being "completely mystified" by the entire Allende affair, he agreed with Jessup's analysis that there seemed to be "too much in these letters to ignore them wholly." "UFOlogy", wrote Sanderson, "is a truly funny business. It cannot be all bunkum; yet some of its implications are so bizarre as to be almost beyond comprehension." Summing it all up, he concluded that he felt the mystery of the Allende affair "more worthy of further investigation than any other I have come across."

CHAPTER 4

Some Clues and a Few Conjectures

Did the so-called Philadelphia Experiment really happen? During the years since Jessup's death the controversy has continued to rage, occasionally enhanced by bits of new evidence, but with the basic mystery remaining unsolved. Certainly a story of such strange and bizarre proportions would not just fade away regardless of circumstances. But with the passing of the man who was the obvious central figure in the affair up to this point, the perplexing matter of the Allende letters proceeded quite rapidly (and quite predictably, I suppose) to become something of a legend.

The story seems to have been kept alive by an at first very small but gradually expanding group of believers who, upon examination, seem to fit quite nicely into two different categories: They either had been personally acquainted with Dr. Jessup during his life and hence had some firsthand knowledge of the letters and the

events surrounding them, or they knew someone in the former category who had discussed
the story with them. In any event, interest has
continued unabated right up to the present day,
generally centering around what possible clues,
if indeed any, these letters and the events surrounding them might be able to provide with
respect to the existence and effect of hitherto
supposedly unknown and untapped forms of energy. While Sherby and Hoover's initial involvement seems to have stemmed from their
interest in uncovering possible clues to the secrets of antigravity and UFO propulsion, interest has continued over the years for a whole
variety of reasons, ranging all the way from
simple curiosity to theoretical physics.

Einstein's Unified Field Theory is even today
a misty and little-understood concept. The mysteries that may eventually be unlocked by some
future application of that theory could well be
more staggering to the world than was the development of atomic power from $E = mc^2$. Those
who read Allende's letters and did not reject
them out of hand as mere rubbish or the ravings
of a psychopath—in short, those who took the
trouble to question whether there might possibly be some element of truth in them—found
their minds whirling with speculations about
a host of unfathomable subjects. If in fact the
Navy did somehow succeed, either by accident
or design, in creating force-field invisibility—
or even teleportation (the instantaneous transfer of solid objects from one place to another)—

then, for example, might not the results of such experiments also offer some clues toward explaining the strange series of events and disappearances that seem to plague the area popularly known as the Bermuda Triangle where electromagnetic clouds seem to herald the disappearances of planes or ships? Is there a possibility that these craft, stuck in time and oblivious to its passing, continue to travel to a destination they will never reach? Did the experiment perhaps provide evidence of the existence of other dimensions in time and space? Did it reveal clues to a new and cheap way of travel or energy production, not to mention the fact that in such a fantastic discovery might lie the key to the ultimate secret weapon? The possibilities are both endless and staggering!

But *are* the letters authentic? For if they are not—if they have not even the slightest basis in fact—then they are obviously keys to nothing at all, and all of the hoopla which has been associated with them for the past two decades means nothing.

There seem to be, then, three possibilities: (1) The ship experiment, the Allende letters, and consequently Allende himself are nothing but fakes and frauds and as a consequence should be completely discounted. (2) The letters are a true account of a real event. (3) They are an exaggerated, distorted, and highly sensationalized account of a real event and hence do have some foundation in fact but are only partially true.

If we select option (1), then not only have we closed our minds without proper examination of the evidence, but there is no further need to continue investigating the matter. And if we select either of the other two options, it seems only reasonable and proper to expect that we do so out of reasons based on fact rather than opinion. In spite of the all too frequent initial reaction (even Jessup himself was guilty of it) that this matter is "just too fantastic to believe," the more one tends to think about it, the more it fixes itself within one's mind. While the impulse to dismiss the whole thing as nothing but a hoax (a cruel hoax indeed, for it was fatal for Dr. Jessup) is admittedly illogical, it is at least the most convenient route that one can take out of the affair. For to do otherwise is quickly to discover that this story has a peculiar way of returning to haunt one; of reaching out to ensnare the investigator in a net: Either prove it, or lay it to rest—but do something with it. The merely curious remain interested; the dedicated are trapped.

And so, what began innocently enough as a serious effort to try to disprove the whole thing has blossomed into the book you are now reading. The more one tried to discount the story, the more one found one confronted by evidence that seemed to support it.

Exactly why or how the ship experiment outlined in the Allende letters came to be called the Philadelphia Experiment is not exactly known, although it is certain that the designation is definitely not an official one. As far as is known there has never been a military undertaking of any sort which used that project title. It is more likely that the name arose out of the need of one or more of the early researchers into the matter to call it something; and since at least a portion of the project allegedly took place at the Philadelphia Navy Yard, it seemed only appropriate to refer to the entire affair as the Philadelphia Experiment. In any event, the name stuck, and we might as well continue to use it.

Perhaps what is indicated at this point is a concise summary of the matter we are dealing with. After all, these letters when properly examined do indeed contain a variety of clues in their own right; and these clues set apart by themselves constitute quite a body around which an investigation can be constructed. Research should always start with the basic available information.

Here then is a synopsis of the two surviving Allende letters, including those points which can justifiably be viewed as a basis from which to begin any serious investigation into the matter.

According to Carlos Miguel Allende:

1. Dr. Albert Einstein's Unified Field Theory was in fact completed in 1925–27, but Dr. Einstein withdrew it because he was allegedly "horrified" by the possible uses it might be put

to by a mankind not yet ready for it. This, according to Allende, could be confirmed by "Dr. B. Russell."

(This item constitutes no small matter in itself, for any proper examination of such a statement with an eye toward possible substantiation would seem to require not only a discussion of what the Unified Field Theory is all about, but a reasonably close look into the life and personality of Dr. Einstein as well.)

2. During World War II, the concepts of the Unified Field Theory were tested by the Navy "with a view to any and every possible quick use of it, if feasible, in a very short time." Someone called Dr. Franklin Reno, a man Allende refers to as "my friend," allegedly had something to do with producing "results" at this stage of the game.

3. The "results" thus produced were used to achieve "complete invisibility of a ship, destroyer type, and all of its crew, while at sea (Oct. 1943)" by means of some sort of energy or force field which had been created around the ship. The men on the ship were apparently able to see one another vaguely, but all that could be seen by anyone outside of the field was "the clearly defined shape of the ship's hull in the water." The effects of this invisibility-creating force field upon the men involved were, according to Allende, "disastrous." The experiment, he says, was a complete success, but the men were complete failures.

4. There was a special berth for the experi-

mental ship at the Philadelphia Navy Yard.

5. A small item once appeared in a Philadelphia newspaper which would verify the tale. This supposedly described the "sailors' activities after their initial voyage" when they "raided" a local bar, allegedly the "Seamens Lounge," and where they presumably were either still exhibiting the effects of the field, or proceeded to discuss the experiment in such graphic terms that it terrified the waitresses. One is left to assume that the Shore Patrol was called and that some reporter picked up the story and wrote it up without quite believing it.

6. Allende himself claims to have observed at least portions of this experiment while at sea on board the Liberty Ship *S.S. Andrew Furuseth*, a Matson Lines ship out of Norfolk. This was sometime in October 1943. According to Allende, other men who were on deck at the time and witnessed the tests were: Chief Mate Mowsely; Richard "Splicey" Price, an eighteen- or nineteen-year-old sailor from Roanoke, Virginia; a man named "Connally" from New England (possibly Boston).

7. Rear Admiral Rawson Bennett, Navy Chief of Research, could supposedly verify that the experiment had in fact occurred.

8. The experimental ship also somehow mysteriously disappeared from its Philadelphia dock and showed up only minutes later in the Norfolk area. It then subsequently vanished again only to reappear at its Philadelphia dock. Total elapsed time—a matter of minutes. Al-

The Norfolk port facilities where the *Eldridge* was reported to have materialized after its disappearance from the Philadelphia Navy Yard. (*National Archives*)

The Philadelphia Navy Yard during World War II. This photograph was not declassified until July 12, 1977. (*National Archives*)

lende says he only heard about this phase of it, and that this may have been as late as 1946 "after the experiments were discontinued."

9. Allende indicates that the Office of Naval Research was under the direction of "the present [at the time of the letter—1956] boss of the Navy, Burke" at the time that the force-field experiments were conducted, and that it was because of his "curiosity and willingness and prompting that this experiment was enabled to be carried out." This Burke is described by Allende as a man who possessed a very positive attitude toward research.

10. Finally, in addition to his then current address, Allende also supplies Jessup with the following data about himself: his presumed merchant sailor's Z number, Z416175; the fact that he served on the *S.S. Andrew Furuseth* for some six months; and that he considers himself as "something of a dialectician" and "stargazer" and in addition he travels a great deal "around the country."

Obviously the research needed to run down and substantiate all of these items not only constitutes a considerable undertaking, but is equally predicated on the successful discovery of substantial additional information as well as the willing, if not outright friendly, cooperation of quite a large number of people along the way.

Did the Philadelphia Experiment really happen the way Allende says it did? And if so, what are the implications with regard to the discovery and utilization of as yet undreamed-of forms of energy—energy of a type and form which, as Allende suggests, might well be the power source utilized by those strange aerial objects which we refer to as UFOs?

Worthy of recall at this point are Allende's closing remarks at the end of the third letter with respect to this subject: "Perhaps the Navy has used this accident of transport to build your UFOs. It is a logical advance from any stand-point."

Logical? Possibly; but before we can begin to offer possible answers to this question, we should first turn our attention to the character who seems at this point to be squarely in the center of this entire mysterious affair—Señor Carlos Miguel Allende.

CHAPTER 5

The Mysterious
Señor Allende

Although numerous attempts have been made
by other researchers over the years to solve the
mystery posed by the Allende letters, virtually
all of them have stopped short of producing any
evidence of real value because of their inability
to produce the key to the whole affair: the elusive Carlos Allende himself. It was generally
assumed that since Allende had written the letters, the only way to solve the mystery was to
find him and add his firsthand testimony to the
record. Failure to ferret out this witness resulted in an endless set of conjectures, but little
else.

The problem was further complicated by several "fake" Allendes who surfaced during the
1960s offering to "sell the story" if the price was
right. One of these even went so far as to have
his letters postmarked in New Kensington—the

real Allende's supposed hometown. Fortunately, not one of the prospective buyers was convinced. Some even doubted that there was a real Carlos, and asserted that the whole thing was really a plot cooked up by Naval Intelligence to discredit private UFO research—an interesting hypothesis, but one which is unsupported by the complex facts of the matter.

The problems encountered in trying to locate Allende were considerable. Laborious and time-consuming checks of telephone directories in various cities and rural areas, checks of military, naval and merchant marine records, police and newspaper files, obituaries, and queries to writers and researchers of unexplained phenomena were unsuccessful, until an unusual coincidence provided the answer.

It came through Jim Lorenzen, one of the first persons contacted. Lorenzen, who is the director of the Aerial Phenomenon Research Organization (A.P.R.O.) in Tucson, Arizona, said that the *A.P.R.O. Journal* had carried a story on Allende in 1969 after a man claiming to be Allende had turned up at A.P.R.O. headquarters and had made certain "confessions" (later repudiated) during an interview concerning his allegations about the Philadelphia Experiment. Lorenzen was kind enough to send a copy of a photograph he had taken of Allende during the interview, but was unable to provide anything beyond that because he hadn't heard from Allende since and had no address. But about a month later, Moore again got in touch with Lorenzen on a different matter. Jim's answer was several weeks in arriving, but when it came, attached to the bottom of it as a sort of P.S. was the unexpected phrase: "In today's mail came a letter from C.A." followed by an address. Although the address was not Allende's, the trail it provided was now fresh enough to follow, and eventually contact was made.

While finding Allende was certainly a step in the right direction in researching the "Philadelphia Experiment," getting anything concrete out of him on that topic was quite another problem. Although maintaining contact with the man who calls himself Carlos Allende has produced voluminous correspondence, several lengthy telephone conversations and a couple of face-to-face meetings, it is still virtually impossible to say very much about him with any great degree of certainty.

Allende is about six feet tall, balding, spare of frame and usually somewhat shabbily dressed. His eyes often show suspicion, but he occasionally smiles gently. He is given to rambling monologues about his thoughts on many topics besides the Philadelphia Experiment. When he does talk about the Philadelphia Experiment, he often appears to be keeping something back or avoiding a direct answer. When pressed for information, he will change the subject. He will make appointments, then not show up, or will appear unannounced.

Carlos Miguel Allende (or Carl Allen). (*APRO*)

Just who is Allende really? Aside from the fact that he is known to use no fewer than five different aliases, he certainly seems to be the same person who corresponded with Dr. Jessup. Not only is his peculiar style of writing similar to that found in the Allende Letters, but he still has what he says is one of the original postcards written to him by Dr. Jessup in 1956. Anything else about him however is open to conjecture; and in actuality there seem to be at least two very distinct possibilities concerning his real identity.

The first of these, based on information coming mostly from Carlos Allende himself, has it that he was born "Carl Allen," the youngest of three children of an Irish father and a Gypsy mother, on May 31, 1925, on a farm outside of a small Pennsylvania town (not New Kensington). Of his early life not much is known save that the family lived on a small farm and that young Carlos (or Carl) quit school "in his ninth year." We are told he was a moody and rather restless youngster who liked to lose himself in books.

On Tuesday, July 14, 1942, six weeks after his seventeenth birthday, he left a life of farm work and odd jobs to join the Marine Corps. He had served only ten months, however, when he was discharged on Friday, May 21, 1943, at Charleston, South Carolina, "upon report of medical survey for disability." Following a brief visit home, he went to Philadelphia, where he enlisted in the Merchant Marine in July of that same year. A few days later he received orders to proceed immediately to Seamen's Training School at Hoffman Island, New York.

His first assignment, and the one we are interested in, was serving under Ship's Master W.S. Dodge as a member of the deck crew of the *S.S. Andrew Furuseth*, a Liberty Ship which sailed from Norfolk bound for Casablanca, North Africa, on August 16, 1943. He was to stay with that ship for a little over five months, until late January 1944, when he left the *Furuseth* to sign on as a crewman on the *S.S. Newton D. Baker* (thus clearly placing the date of the Philadelphia Experiment project within this time frame).

Allende served on some twenty-seven different ships in both the Atlantic and Pacific until October 1952, when, having become disgruntled by Seamen's Union disputes which seemed to be denying him further ship assignments, he left the sea for good in search of better fortune elsewhere.

Beyond this, his life is pretty much a mystery save for what has already been written concerning his involvement with Dr. Jessup and his subsequent "confession" to APRO. He proceeded to wander about the country and the world in true gypsy fashion, seeking, as he put it, "odd jobs and education" from whatever opportunities came his way. He succeeded in obtaining both while seeing a great deal of the world in the process. We find he spent considerable time in the middle 1950s working haphazardly for a number of well-drilling outfits throughout western Texas and eastern New Mexico. He was indeed in Seminole, Texas, when the strange annotated book was mailed from there to Admiral Furth, and he was also in the Gainesville, Texas, vicinity at about the time the second Allende letter was received by Dr. Jessup—substantiating his connection with both documents.

A drifter, he nonetheless apparently became worried when the Navy and others began taking an interest in him following his contacts with Dr. Jessup, and he "went into hiding" for a number of years. He finally ended up in the Los Altos region of southern-central Mexico (interestingly in about the same general area where Jessup's mysterious craters were located), and eventually he came to consider the region his home. He had been to the area before during the course of his wanderings, and claims that in fact it was the gypsies of this region who "Mexicanized" Carl Allen into Carlos Miguel Allende. At the time of this writing he is still living there.

As for his story, this might all be very well and one might have been inclined to believe it without question had not a remarkable series

SERIAL NUMBER

A 103664

B

UNITED STATES
BUREAU OF MAR

CERTIFICATE O

This is to certify that Carl

18 years of age, born in Pennsy

States Board of

wall of which

hearing and ph

as a result of sa

mitting him

hereby rated as

Signature of Seaman

Certificate issued to Able Seaman Carl Allen showing the "Z" number
he used in his letters to Dr. Jessup.

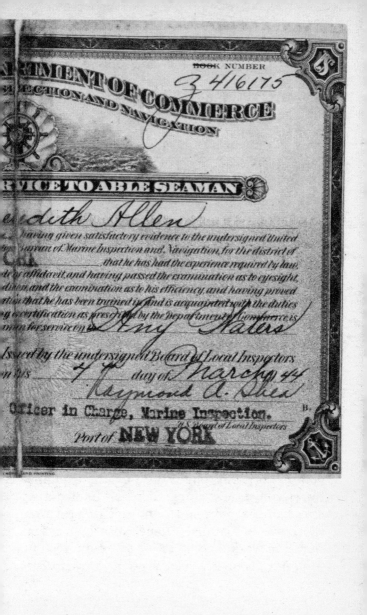

BOOK NUMBER

3 416175

...RTMENT OF COMMERCE
...SPECTION AND NAVIGATION

...RVICE TO ABLE SEAMAN

...edith Allen

...having given satisfactory evidence to the undersigned United
...Bureau of Marine Inspection and Navigation, for the district of
...CA._____ that he has had the experience required by law,
...by affidavit, and having passed the examination as to eyesight,
...tion, and the examination as to his efficiency, and having proved
...tion that he has been trained in and is acquainted with the duties
...certification as prescribed by the Department of Commerce, is
...man for service on the Any Waters

...Issued by the undersigned Board of Local Inspectors
...this ___7th___ day of ___March___ 44

Raymond A. Shea

Officer in Charge, Marine Inspection.

B.

U.S. Board of Local Inspectors

Port of **NEW YORK**

of circumstances intervened to cast an entirely new light on the matter.

Some years ago, during the course of some research, Moore managed to stumble quite by accident upon the fact that there was indeed an Allende family living in western Pennsylvania during the period of the early and middle 1950s at about the same time that Carlos Allende was giving his home address as New Kensington, Pennsylvania. Since the name Allende is not an especially common one in Pennsylvania, a closer examination of this strange coincidence seemed almost essential and was undertaken immediately. The results are revealing in light of Carlos' own story.

It seems that sometime following World War II, two brothers named Allende came to America from Puerto Rico seeking work. The exact story is unclear, but somehow or other the elder brother, Pedro, who had settled for a time in Clairton, Pa., happened to hear that a certain Mrs. Blockson, a lady from his home town in Puerto Rico, had made her home in the suburban Pittsburgh community of Sewickley. Believing that this lady might be able to help him obtain work, he sought her out and explained his circumstances. Mrs. Blockson immediately asked to see his hands, and upon discovering the hard and callused hands of a man accustomed to work, agreed to try to obtain a job for him. Arrangements were soon made, and Pedro took up residence with his wife and small children (one of whom, coincidentally, is living today under the name of Allen) in a small two-story frame home which was located in a rural area of Aleppo Township, Glenfield, Pennsylvania. A few months later, he had accumulated enough to make a small down payment on the property.

It is the appearance on the scene of the second brother, Felicito, or Filo, Allende, that begins a series of most bizarre coincidences. According to Mrs. Blockson, both brothers had come originally from the town of Hato Rey in Puerto Rico, where their father had been employed by the first big power plant on that island, located at the falls of the Comerío River. Filo was quite a few years junior to Pedro, but, although he had quit school "in his ninth year" (third grade), spoke better English because he had served in the U.S. Merchant Marine during World War II. He came to Glenfield only briefly in the early 1950s to visit his brother, and is described as a drifter type who couldn't stay put. He spoke both Spanish and English (as does Carlos Allende), was strictly self-educated and very well read. Obviously there is no further need to go on underlining the points of similarity, since they must already be more than apparent by this time. But to continue:

Mrs. Blockson goes on to characterize Filo as a character who "generally didn't talk much, but when he did would go off on some seemingly unimportant issue and speak at great lengths on it. He was a loner who didn't work much but who would habitually go off to parts unknown, frequently without even bothering to tell anyone he was going, and would be gone for days, weeks or months at a time without word. His attitude toward humanity and God seemed rather negative." Also, he may have "used names other than his own."

Anyhow, Filo's occasional visits to his brother's home continued in this manner until about mid-1954, when tragedy struck the family in the form of a freak accident. Pedro, while up on a ladder doing some repair work on the house, chanced to miss a step and fell heavily to the ground, striking his head. Although the external wounds healed normally, severe internal damage had been done. Pedro was forced to quit work indefinitely. The family, which had never been more than a hair's breadth ahead of poverty in the best of times, soon began to feel the pinch. And to make matters worse, Filo, whose help might have made the difference in these circumstances, was off on another of his extended "travels" and knew nothing of the affair. Pedro, unable to afford adequate medical care, lived on at home, becoming increasingly deranged as time went on.

And so it went for some months until 2:15 A.M. on the morning of Thursday, May 19, 1955, when Burgess R.W. Cook of Glenfield received a call for police from a neighbor of the Allendes' who reported that Pedro Allende was chasing his wife with a hammer. Cook immediately alerted the Allegheny County Police, and a car was dispatched to the scene. Before it could arrive, however, Cook received a second urgent call from the same neighbor, this reporting that the Allende house was on fire. Poor Pedro, now completely out of his senses, had set fire to the curtains.

The Allendes had lost virtually all they owned. Mrs. Allende was taken to Sewickley Valley Hospital suffering from shock. The four children, the youngest barely two years old, were split among neighbors and friends, and Pedro was taken to the Pennsylvania State Hospital for the Mentally Insane at Woodville. He died soon afterward, allegedly from the effects of another fall—this time in a bathtub.

Meanwhile, Mrs. Allende had succeeded in reuniting herself with her children, and had moved to a modest apartment in another town.

The story, however, is not yet over. Within days after the funeral, the errant Filo again appeared on the scene. He had been away for nearly a year (it was now mid-June 1955), and he was totally unaware of what had happened in his absence. Greatly disturbed at finding charred ruins where his brother's house should have been, and unable to learn anything but the barest of details from the neighbors, he made his way to Mrs. Blockson's home in nearby Sewickley to seek an explanation. It was there that he learned the details of the tragic event. He remained in the area only a day or two, visibly upset and keeping to himself the whole time, and then, without warning or word, quietly vanished without a trace—never to be heard from by family or friends again. Only a few short months later Morris Jessup received the first of a series of three letters from a man calling himself Carlos Miguel Allende.

Are Carlos and Filo Allende the same person? No one but Carlos knows for sure, and he isn't telling. Mrs. Blockson, who knew Filo reasonably well by sight, did examine the photo of Carlos Allende that appears in this book, but was unable to state with any degree of certainty whether the man in the photo is Filo Allende. Carlos himself, when asked the question directly, made an uncharacteristically brief reply: "I do not choose to answer that question at this time." In light of this, we are left with nothing more than an intriguing series of coincidences and some rather tantalizing similarities in dates and places.

One researcher has even gone as far as to suggest, quite seriously, that Filo Allende met and befriended a real Carl Allen while in the Merchant Marine. Later, when this Allen met with an accident of some sort, Filo simply assumed his identity for reasons known only to himself. Admittedly this is sheer speculation; but in the absence of clear facts, it's as good an explanation as any other.

In any event, regardless of Allende's real identity, the point of supreme importance in all this still remains: What can this individual tell us about the alleged Philadephia Experiment that can help us solve the mystery? Alas, to the complete dismay of all the earlier researchers who have pinned their hopes for a solution upon finding him, he actually knows pitifully little beyond what he has already written on the topic in his letters to Jessup.

The truth is that Allende was not a scientist, nor even a trained observer, but merely a deck-hand who happened to be in the right (or wrong?) place at the proper time to view a sight which he was (and still is) totally at a loss to explain. Did he see a ship vanish? According to his own testimony, he did. How was it done? He doesn't know exactly, but it had to do with force fields of some sort. "There was plenty of static electricity associated with it." Could he name the ship? Yes, he could: "It was the DE 173." Did he see it vanish more than once? No, he didn't. "But it did," he adds knowingly. Where did he obtain his information on Einstein, Russell, and Admiral Bennett? "From friends in high places who shall go nameless." Dr. Einstein, he maintains, actually witnessed parts of the experiment. Also, Allende says he saw a man "vanish" from sight while standing on a loading dock, but he can't recall the date or what dock it was.

A part of his own account to Moore of some of these events follows in his own words:

So you want to know about Einstein's great experiment, Eh? Do you know...I actually shoved my hand, up to the elbow, into this unique force field as that field flowed, surging powerfully in a *counter*clockwise direction around the little experimental Navy ship, the DE 173. I felt the ...push of that force field against the solidness of my arm and hand outstretched into its humming-pushing-propelling flow.

I watched the air all around the ship...turn slightly, ever so slightly, darker than all the other air...I saw, after a few minutes, a foggy green mist arise like a thin cloud.* [I think] this must have been a mist of atomic particles. I watched as thereafter the DE 173 became rapidly invisible to human eyes. And yet, the precise shape of the keel and under-hull of that...ship *remained* impressed into the ocean water as it and my own ship sped

---

*This account closely resembles reports from survivors or observers of disappearances within the Bermuda Triangle, where the aberration may represent a natural (or unnatural) phenomenon on a larger scale.

along somewhat side by side and close to in-boards. Yes, today I can tell it, but then, who cares?...

...in trying to describe the sounds that [the] force field made as it circled around the DE 173...it began as a humming sound, quickly built up...to a humming whispering sound, and then increased to a strongly sizzling buzz—[like a] rushing torrent...

The field had a *sheet* of pure electricity around it as it flowed. [This]...flow was strong enough to almost knock me completely off balance and had my entire body been within that field, the flow would of a most absolute certainty [have] knocked me flat...on my own ship's deck. As it was, my entire body was *not* within that force field when it reached maximum strength-density, repeat, *density*, and so I was not knocked down but my arm and hand was [sic] only pushed backward with the field's flow.

Why was I not electrocuted the instant my bare hand touched that...sheet of electricity surrounding the field flow? It must have been because...[I was wearing] hip-high rubber sailor's boots and sou'wester coat.

...Naval ONR scientists today do not yet understand what took place that day. They say the field was "reversed." Scientific history, I later came to realize, was made for the first time that day.

As for the rest of it, he is totally unshakable in his story concerning the newspaper articles which he says he saw while on leave in Philadelphia, and he admits to only slightly embellishing his tale of the experiment's effects on the sailors—a tale which he says he pieced together mostly from dockside scuttlebutt. He did this, he says, because he was worried that Jessup would succeed in influencing the government to accelerate research into the Unified Field Theory, and he wanted to scare him off if possible. Based on what he had witnessed and heard, he feared the results of such research, if placed in the wrong hands, would bring an end to society as we know it.

Nonetheless, all of this boils down to the simple fact that while Carlos may have started the controversy that has raged on over the so-called Philadelphia Experiment for more than two decades, he really doesn't appear to have the essential information needed to solve the mystery. Did it really happen? Allende maintains it did, but even he can't prove it.

The possibility that Allende himself might have been the strange little man who related the bizarre story to airmen Davis and Huse in a Colorado Springs park in 1970 (see Chapter I) seems to be without foundation. In their interviews, both men stated with certainty that they felt they would be able to recognize the man they had met if they were ever to see him again, yet neither of them was able to identify the photograph of Allende as the character in question. If this man wasn't Allende, then the question of who he may have been becomes even more intriguing and may, perhaps, open other doors.

CHAPTER 6

Investigations Can Be Fatal

After the initial shock effect of the Allende letters wears off and one takes the time for a closer and more objective evaluation, a number of curious things about their contents begin to come to light. Perhaps the most noticeable of these is the fact that Allende seems to go out of his way to mention a number of people in them—people whom he says can "verify" his story. In all there are nine such individuals mentioned, although one is not named but only described. Those that are named are as follows:

1. Dr. Albert Einstein
2. "Dr. B. Russell"
3. "my friend Dr. Franklin Reno"
4. "Chief Mate Mowsely" of the *S.S. Furuseth*
5. Richard "Splicey" Price, crew member
6. "Connally," also a crew member
7. Rear Admiral Rawson Bennett
8. "the present boss of the Navy Burke"

The first two, Dr. Einstein and Dr. B. Russell, are widely recognized by their names alone. Dr. B. Russell can be none other than Bertrand Russell, the eminent writer, philosopher, humanitarian, and pacifist who, in his later years, did indeed befriend Dr. Einstein to the extent that intimate discussions took place between them—which conceivably could have included discussion of how possible misuses of some of Einstein's theories could result in irreparable threats to mankind's very existence. How Carlos Allende might have found out about these discussions, if in fact they did occur, is anybody's guess. Einstein himself and his Unified Field Theory will be the topic of a separate chapter in this book.

Identifying the third man on the list was not quite as simple a matter. A considerable amount of research and investigatory work was required before it could be reliably established that Carlos Allende did indeed have contact with a very real Dr. Franklin Reno. The mystery, however, is hardly diminished by the discovery that the name itself is actually a pseudonym. The story surrounding this important discovery and the information subsequently uncovered is, to say the least, a lengthy one and in order to do justice to it, it must also be deferred to a separate chapter.

Unfortunately similar successes cannot be claimed concerning the next three names, all of whom Carlos Allende claims were sailors aboard the *S.S. Furuseth* and witnesses to the

Philadelphia Experiment. Although the chief mate of the *Furuseth* was indeed one Arthur Maudsley, a wall of silence has been met in all efforts to obtain any information from this individual concerning his service aboard that ship—a silence that in itself might be construed as most revealing.

Even less can be said about Richard "Splicey" Price of Roanoke, Virginia, and "Connally" of New England. Concerning Price, a brief investigation turned up reasonably reliable information that he died in 1973. As for Connally (whose first name, by the way, appears to have been Frank or Peter), needless to say there are probably several score of them in the New England area—if indeed the one we would be looking for still lives there.

Since the crew records of the *Furuseth* no longer exist, it is difficult to come up with anything definite regarding others who might have served on that ship with Allende, but persistent research has turned up the names of three other possible crew members—none of whom the authors have thus far been able to locate. These are Hermann C. Schultz, who apparently was the ship's bosun; William Reilly (or Ripley?); and Lewis Vincent. All of these were from the New York–New England area. Reilly may have been a professional musician, Vincent was a New England fisherman, and Schultz was a longtime merchant sailor.

As for Admiral Rawson Bennett II, whom Allende refers to in his second letter as "Navy

Chief [sic] of research" and whom he admonishes Jessup to "contact...for verification of info. herein," a most curious fact emerges when we examine this further, which leads us to wonder just exactly where Allende *did* get his information. The strange thing is that while Bennett was indeed chief of the Office of Naval Research at the time Dr. Jessup received Allende's second letter (January 13, 1956), he had been so only since January 1, when he had replaced Admiral Frederick R. Furth (the "Admiral N. Furth" to whom Allende had sent the annotated copy of Jessup's book some months earlier). Since Allende must have posted his letter considerably earlier for Jessup to have received it via his publisher on January 13, the question becomes: How did Allende know that Bennett had replaced Furth as chief of ONR? The fact that this letter was postmarked Gainesville, Texas, makes the matter even more perplexing, since while such an event might have been barely newsworthy enough to have made an obscure page in *The Washington Post* or *The New York Times* on a slow day, it would hardly have been the sort of thing any of the Texas newspapers would bother with. Such changes of command are virtually everyday affairs in Washington military circles and hardly make for earthshaking news even locally, much less half a continent away.

But if Allende's source of information was close to the top, he seems to slip up quite badly with the last name on the list. His identification of "the present boss of the Navy Burke" as having been Chief of Naval Research at the time of the alleged Philadelphia Experiment was completely erroneous. Although there was indeed a real Admiral Arleigh A. Burke, he had virtually nothing to do with Navy Research either during World War II or thereafter. Burke commanded a destroyer squadron in the Pacific in 1943 during the time of the alleged Philadelphia Experiment, and in fact seems to have been a fleet officer almost throughout his Navy career.

Allende's error may have been a human one, however; for if we read the description he gives of "Burke" in his third letter to Jessup, we find that this individual is characterized as a man of "curiosity and willingness and prompting" and that it was "his attitude toward advanced and ultra-advanced types of research" that was responsible for his rise to the rank of admiral. Curiously enough the man who fits this description was not Admiral *Burke* but Admiral Harold G. *Bowen*—who not only was director of the Naval Research Laboratory at the time of the inception of the Philadelphia Experiment project, but was also the prime mover responsible for a whole host of Top Secret "ultra-advanced types" of projects during World War II! However, while the similarity of the names may possibly account for Allende's confusion on this matter, it does not explain how his information could be so pinpoint accurate on the one account (with regard to Admiral Bennett) and so far off the mark on the other—unless, of course, he felt the need to conceal the name of the person to whom he was referring.

No search for clues in a matter such as this could possibly be complete without at least a brief examination of what other researchers have published on this topic. As was noted at the beginning of this work, although the matter of the Philadelphia Experiment has been lurking in the periphery of research efforts into the unknown for the past two decades, it has not gone entirely without its champions. Admittedly the literature on the topic is sparse, but what there is of it is well worth examining.

Perhaps the earliest attempt to bring some of the mystery to light through the printed page was made by Dr. Reilly H. Crabb, an acquaintance of Dr. Jessup's and currently director of the Borderland Sciences Research Foundation of Vista, California. BSRF, among other things, publishes a collection of small and relatively inexpensive tracts on various topics of esoteric interest; and although most of these have been of extremely limited circulation, some are quite interesting. The appearance of one of these early in 1962 under the title *M.K. Jessup, the Allende Letters and Gravity,* edited by Crabb himself, seems to have sparked a great deal of the controversy which followed. At the same time it also provided invaluable primary source material for anyone interested in doint further research into the affair. In it Crabb published for the first time in a civilian source not only the two surviving Allende letters, but also several pages in facsimile of the Varo annotated edition of Jessup's book *The Case for the UFO*.

Briefly stated, Crabb's conjectures on the Philadelphia Experiment as set forth in this booklet center around his belief that T. Townsend Brown, a noted physicist and antigravity researcher, had at the very least something to do with the invisibility project while head of a department under the Bureau of Ships in the Navy, and that in fact (according to Crabb) the whole thing might actually have been Brown's idea. Brown was involved with the project, but it wasn't his idea, as we shall see later.

Closely following Crabb's lead in the matter came Gray Barker, flying saucer researcher, and a local publisher working out of Clarksburg, West Virginia. Relying largely on information gleaned from Crabb, but adding some of his own, Barker took the initiative in 1963 in publishing what is still regarded today as one of the most valuable works on the topic of the Allende letters: *The Strange Case of Dr. M.K. Jessup* (Clarksburg, West Virginia: Saucerian Press, 1963). Unlike Crabb, who seems to have published his tract mostly as a service to interested BSRF members and associates, Barker was actually interested enough in the mystery to try to discover a few answers on his own.

Although Barker's book doesn't do much in the way of providing clues toward solving the mystery, it does provide considerable background information on Jessup himself, including excerpts from several of his more obscure articles and letters. Also noted is the fact that no autopsy was ever performed on Dr. Jessup because of his desire that his body be used for scientific purposes. Final cremation, we are told, took place on January 30, 1962.

The one other item of interest in Barker's book is his reproduction of a rather curious letter which Barker claims to have received from an anonymous source known to him only as "Colonel B." While admonishing us that the designation "Colonel" is "not necessarily to be construed as representing a military commission or degree," the "Colonel" does indeed make some interesting points. An excerpt from this letter follows:

...It will be indeed unfortunate if you make too much of a mystery out of the suicide of Dr. Jessup.

When I met Jessup in 1958, his mind seemed to be occupied with gaining proof as to the authenticity of certain psychic claims...

He also made a great deal of emphasis on a mimeographed version of one of his books, allegedly circulated in the Armed Services. He also told me of certain letters he had received purporting to contain information about a secret experiment by the military, involving an application of the Unified Field Theory.

I personally feel that too much was made

of this by Jessup, though this can be understandable when one considers it in the light of the sensitivity shown in government circles about the UFO investigation. It is my educated guess that the allegations contained in [these] letters regarding secret experiments were hoaxes of some sort. Yet because this information *DID COME CLOSE* [emphasis his] to some of the circumstances of *ACTUAL* experiments (of a much less dramatic nature), it may have been thought that there had been some security leak and this may very likely have been the reason for the great interest by the military.

Even though I could make an educated guess as to the nature of the actual experiments, I certainly do not feel it would be in order to do so....

Whoever this mysterious informant might have been, he certainly came closer to the truth of this matter than almost anyone else—as we shall come to see.

Through the years it has been largely through the efforts of Gray Barker and his small but persistent Saucerian Press operation that the mystery surrounding Jessup and the Allende letters has been kept alive—and this in spite of the fact that his books have had a limited circulation. But perhaps his greatest contribution came in the summer of 1973 when, as we have already mentioned, he succeeded in obtaining a nearly mint copy of the Varo annotated edition of *The Case for the UFO* and published and sold it in a limited edition of 500 facsimile copies. After seventeen years of whispers and rumors about the document's existence, Barker finally succeeded in bringing the matter into the light of day.

The first attempt to link Allende's account of the events of the Philadelphia Experiment (and other force-field phenomena in general) to the weird and inexplicable events of what we today tend to refer to as the Bermuda Triangle was made in a 1964 book by Vincent Gaddis entitled *Invisible Horizons*. By and large the book itself is an excellently researched and detailed study of some of the strange disappearances and other unexplained events which have occurred at sea over the past few hundred years, and is highly recommended to anyone interested in this particular topic. It is the last chapter of this book that we are interested in, however; for in this chapter (entitled "Is There an Answer?") Gaddis suggests that the frightening results of the Philadelphia Experiment might provide clues to what was behind some of the other more fully documented but equally perplexing cases of ships and crews that disappeared while at sea.

During the course of this chapter Gaddis also happens to add a few hitherto unpublished clues of his own which presumably constitute the fruit of his own researches into the matter. Among these appeared the following interesting item (p. 219): "Did Jessup ever have further contact with Allende? We do not know. From some source, however, he apparently did secure some additional information. He told friends that a man went to the Navy and said, in effect: 'You want camouflage, gentlemen! Give me a ship and I'll show you perfect camouflage.' When this man went aboard the experimental ship, he was carrying a black box."

Gaddis also reports, apparently on the basis of an interview with Gray Barker on the topic, that "a close friend of Jessup's . . . is said to have documents 'which might solve the mystery'," and that his "friend" had once tried to find Allende without success.

Gaddis' book, which generally tended to ask questions rather than provide answers, was far from the last word on the topic. In 1967, the controversy was suddenly stirred up again by a new and relatively sensational writer on things unexplained who called himself Brad Steiger. In the final analysis, Steiger (real name: Olson) really had nothing new to offer in the matter. His interest rather derived from the fact that during the course of his investigations of strange phenomena he had happened to run into someone who had a microfilm copy of the Varo annotated edition of Jessup's book. Amazed at what he read and realizing that he might have stumbled on a potential hot potato, Steiger created a rather sensationalized account of the story which was published, along with several reproductions of actual pages from the Varo edition, in the November 1967 issue of *Saga* magazine.

Carlos Allende, as chance would have it, read this account and was considerably stirred by it. Looking into it a bit further, Allende soon discovered that Steiger, together with Florida occultist and researcher Joan W. O'Connell, was in the process of publishing a UFO-oriented book which would include this particular version of the story as one of its chapters. Worried that the book might set the Navy on his trail again, and not wishing publicity in any event, Allende fired off several angry letters to Steiger's publisher asking that the material be suppressed. He was unsuccessful. Not only did the book appear on the shelves, but the publisher had actually added Allende's name to the title! The new book, called *The Allende Letters, New UFO Breakthrough,* appeared in 1968. Allende, who by this time had gone into hiding, steamed on in silence.

Somewhat earlier, in 1967, Dr. Jessup's friend Ivan Sanderson had published a book entitled *Uninvited Visitors*, in which *he* discussed the affair (although again adding nothing new save for his opinion that "after many years of just such 'research' I feel that this 'bit' is more worthy of further investigation than any other I have come across").

By this time Allende was enraged at the unwanted publicity (although an admirer of Sanderson himself), and furious that others were busily making a profit on his story while he himself was nearly penniless. He apparently hit on a plan of revenge: He would admit it was all a hoax. Not only would such an action serve to embarrass and discredit those who had caused him the problem, but it would also diminish their book sales.

Thus resolved, Carlos Miguel Allende walked into the headquarters of the Aerial Phenomena Research Organization (APRO, the oldest and most influential of the UFO research organizations) in Tucson, Ariz., in June 1969, and "confessed all."

Both his letters to Dr. Jessup and the annotations of the Varo edition were hoaxes, he said, designed specifically to "scare the hell out of Jessup." Interestingly, although unknown to the APRO people, he had first gone to Varo itself and proceeded to shake down then corporate president Austin Stanton for a copy of what he said was "his book" (the Varo Ed.), as well as a small payment designed to "get him out of [their] hair." Thus armed, he went to Tucson and it was this copy of the annotated edition of *The Case for the UFO* that he presented to Jim Lorenzen of APRO with the following "confession" added to the top of the second page of the Appendix:

"All words, phrases, and sentences underlined on the following pages in brown ink are false. The below page and the top part of the following were and are the carzyest [sic] pack of lies I ever wrote. Object? To *encourage* ONR

Research and to *discourage* Proffessor [sic] Morris K. Jessup from going further with investigations possibly leading to actual research. *Then* I feared invisibility and force-field research; I don't *now*."

For all its apparent bravado, however, Allende's confession purposely falls short of saying that the Philadelphia Experiment itself was a hoax, for the placement of the "confession" in the Varo edition is neatly done and worded so as to exclude that part of his letter to Jessup which states that such a thing *did* occur. In fact, Lorenzen (who spoke with Allende for over an hour in the privacy of a parked automobile) himself states that "Allende still believes...that a U.S. vessel...disappeared from its Philadelphia dock and reappeared seconds later in the Norfolk-Portsmouth area, then disappeared again to appear once more in its original berth." Allende suggested, he went on, "that the incident could be verified by contacting sailors who were assigned to the ship at the time—some of whom he served with and knew personally." The only part of the letters actually included in the so-called "confession" was the one page and part of the next which dealt with the bizarre aftereffects of the experiment upon the crew members of the ship.

With his plot now hatched and the seeds of his revenge sown (or so he thought), Allende again disappeared from public view.

He later completely repudiated his confession, but for the time being, the ruse worked.

In 1971 when Paris Flammonde, producer of the "Long John Nebel Show" in New York for many years, spoke of the events surrounding Jessup's death, he failed even to so much as mention anything concerning the Allende affair. And in fact, with the exception of another book by Steiger, *Mysteries of Time and Space* (New York: Dell, 1974), most of the other authors who bothered to mention the topic at all spoke disparagingly about it. (See, for example, F.H. Salisbury, *The Utah UFO Display;* and Vincent Sladek, *The New Apocrypha.*) and so it went until mid-1975 when, with the release of worldwide best seller *The Bermuda Triangle,* the entire question was reopened.

This new account of the Jessup-Allende affair approached the problem from an entirely new angle. It contained the one essential item in this matter which no one else up to that point had been able to supply: a witness!

The breakthrough came in the person of Dr. J. Manson Valentine, an oceanographer, zoologist, archaeologist, and longtime (since 1945) student of the Bermuda Triangle, and a close friend of Dr. Jessup's during the time that Jessup had resided in Florida.

Jessup, feeling increasingly depressed and in need of someone to talk to, had spent a great deal of time with Dr. Valentine in the months before his tragic death, and it was during the course of these conversations that he had seen fit to confide to him many of his private thoughts and feelings concerning the Philadelphia Experiment. In fact, Valentine was very possibly the last person to talk to Jessup before his death. He had spoken with his friend during the day on April 20, 1959, and during the course of the conversation had invited Jessup to come to dinner that evening. Jessup accepted, but never arrived.

"Why," he was asked, "did Jessup kill himself?" Valentine's answer was unexpected and startling. "*If* he committed suicide," said Valentine, "it was probably due to extreme depression. He had been approached by the Navy to continue working on the Philadelphia Experiment or similar projects but had declined[!]— he was worried about its dangerous ramifications . . . perhaps he could have been saved. He was still alive when he was found. . . . *Perhaps he was allowed to die.*"

Valentine stated that Jessup had researched the question of the Philadelphia Experiment "pretty thoroughly." "You must remember," he observed, "that he was not a 'crank' writer, but a distinguished and famous scientist." Valentine recollects Jessup telling him some very strange things about what he had learned concerning this incredible project. The experiment, he said, had been accomplished by using naval-type magnetic generators, known as degaussers, which were "pulsed" at resonant frequencies so as to "create a tremendous magnetic field on and around a docked vessel."

Dr. Valentine is of the opinion that Jessup was well informed about the actuality of the

Philadelphia Experiment and had had several conferences with Navy officers and Navy-employed scientists on the subject. He once commented to Valentine: "The experiment is very interesting but awfully dangerous. It is too hard on the people involved. This use of magnetic resonance is tantamount to temporary obliteration in our dimension but it tends to get out of control. Actually it is equivalent to transference of matter into another level or dimension and could represent a dimensional breakthrough if it were possible to control it."

It is highly significant to note that Valentine's account of the experiment, based on information received directly from Dr. Jessup, agreed almost totally with Allende's in that the results of the experiment were "astonishing" but that the crew suffered severe aftereffects. "When the experiment first began to take effect," Valentine recounted, "a hazy green light became evident, something like the reports we have from the survivors of incidents in the Triangle who tell of a luminous green mist. Soon the whole ship was full of this green haze and the craft, together with its personnel, began disappearing from sight of those on the dock until only its waterline was visible." Valentine said that before his death, Jessup believed he was "on the verge of discovering the scientific basis for whatever was happening." The explanation, he felt, was to be found in Einstein's Field Theory.

"In practice," Valentine said, "it concerns

electric and magnetic fields as follows: An electric field created in a coil induces a magnetic field at right angles to the first; each of these fields represents one plane of space. But since there are three planes of space, there must be a third field, perhaps a gravitational one. By hooking up electromagnetic generators so as to produce a magnetic pulse, it might be possible to produce this third field through the principle of resonance. Jessup told me that he thought that the U.S. Navy had inadvertently stumbled on this."

Although only a small section of *Bermuda Triangle* dealt with this topic, the appearance of Dr. Valentine's story created a veritable bombshell, the results of which have yet to subside. Did it really happen? According to Valentine's report about what Dr. Jessup told him then, the evidence seems strongly suggestive. In any event, public pressure on the U.S. Navy for information about the affair has resulted in the creation of a standard form letter which is mailed out routinely to any and all who inquire, and it has been estimated that as much as $2 million has been spent trying to put out the fire sparked by the legend.

One officer succinctly summed up the Navy's problem in dealing with the mounting tide of inquiries by stating that he wished Allende were invisible.

In an apparent effort to throw some cold water on the affair, *Official UFO* magazine published a feature article in its April 1976 issue written by someone calling himself B.R. Strong who claimed to be a close friend of APRO consultant and researcher Kevin D. Randle. Although the story is fairly well written, it is basically a put-down which relies rather heavily on Allende's "APRO confession" coupled with the somewhat one-sided testimony of Captain Sherby, whom Strong reported Randle had found and interviewed at Varo. The article says nothing new, and in fact Allende himself says that several of the statements included in it are nothing but "damn lies." The fact that the *Bermuda Triangle* account is not mentioned at all in the article is not particularly significant, since the article may have been written beforehand.

The subject came up again in Berlitz's recent book, *Without a Trace* (Doubleday, 1977):

Toward the middle of April, 1959, Jessup told Valentine that he had reached what he considered to be some definite conclusions about the series of reactions implied by the Philadelphia Experiment and had *prepared a rough draft he wished to discuss.* Dr. Valentine suggested that he come to dinner. The invitation was for the evening of April 20.

He never came to dinner. At some time before 6:30 P.M., Jessup, according to police reports, drove his car to Matheson's Hammock, a Dade County park . . . and apparently committed suicide. . . . *No notes or manuscript*

DEPARTMENT OF THE NAVY
OFFICE OF INFORMATION
WASHINGTON D.C. 20350

IN REPLY REFER TO
OI-2252A/JVV/dh

2 8 JUL 1976

Over the years we have received innumerable queries about the so-called "Philadelphia Experiment" or "Project" and the alleged role of the Office of Naval Research (ONR) in it. The frequency of these queries predictably intensifies each time the experiment is mentioned by the popular press, often in a science fiction book.

The genesis of the Philadelphia Experiment myth dates back to 1955 with the publication of The Case for UFO's by the late Dr. Morris K. Jessup, a scientist with a Ph.D. in astro-physics and a varied career background.

Form letter sent by the Department of the Navy to persons requesting information about the Philadelphia Experiment.

received a letter by a Carlos Miquel Allende, who gave his address as R.D. #1, Box 223, New Kensington, PA. In the letter, Allende commented on Dr. Jessup's book and gave details of an alleged secret naval experiment in Philadelphia in 1943. During the experiment, according to Allende, a ship was rendered invisible and tele-ported to and from Norfolk in a few minutes, with some terrible after-effects for the crew members. Supposedly, this incredible feat was accomplished by applying Einstein's never-completed "unified field" theory. Allende claimed that he had witnessed the experiment from another ship and that the incident was reported in a Philadelphia newspaper. Neither the identify of Allende, nor that of the newspaper has ever been established.

In 1956 a copy of Jessup's book was mailed anonymously to Admiral Furth, the Chief of Naval Research. The pages of the book were interspersed with hand-written annotations and mar-ginalia apparently made by three different persons as they passed the book back and forth among them. The notations im-plied a knowledge of UFO's, their means of motion and generally, the culture and ethos of the beings occupying these UFO's.

The book came to the attention of two officers then assigned to ONR who happened to have a personal interest in the subject. It was they who contacted Dr. Jessup and asked him to take a look at his book. By the wording and style of one of the writers of the notations, Dr. Jessup concluded that the writer was the same person who had written him about the Philadelphia Experiment. It was also these two officers who personally had the book retyped and who arranged for the publication, in typewritten form, of 25 copies. The officers and their personal belongings have left ONR many years ago, and we do not have even a file copy of the annotated book.

The Office of Naval Research never conducted an official study of the manuscript. As for the Philadelphia Experiment itself, ONR has never conducted any investigations on invisibility, either in 1943 or at any other time. (ONR was established in 1946.) In view of present scientific knowledge, our scientists do not believe that such an experiment could be possible except in the realm of science fiction. A scientific discovery of such import, if it had in fact occurred, could hardly remain secret for such a long time.

I hope this provides a satisfactory answer to your inquiry.

Sincerely,

Betty W. Shirley

BETTY W. SHIRLEY
Head, Research and Public
Inquiries Section

were mentioned in the police report, nor, according to a statement by a witness later given to Dr. Valentine, were any found inside the car.

Berlitz goes on to say in relation to the Philadelphia Experiment itself that "a number of persons in and out of the Navy profess to remember the incident and are even willing to furnish more detailed information about it, except that they are unwilling to be quoted by name"—a situation with which all investigators of this mystery can fully sympathize.

But supposing that such an experiment had been planned and attempted—could it have, even partially, succeeded? An examination of the scientific theory involved might offer a possible solution to this question.

CHAPTER 7

The Einstein Connection

If we are to believe the testimony of both Carlos Allende and Dr. Valentine as previously set forth, then the foundations of the Philadelphia Experiment project are to be discovered in a rather obscure and highly complicated scientific theory first set forth by Dr. Albert Einstein and commonly known as the Unified Field Theory (UFT). Allende, in his second letter to Dr. Jessup, begins by saying that Dr. Einstein first published this theory in the period 1925–27, and that he then "withdrew" it out of concern for what Allende refers to as "humantics." Although Allende does not specifically state just exactly what he means by this strange word "humantics," presumably what he is trying to say is that Dr. Einstein was able to foresee certain possible applications of this theory which he came to fear might somehow be put to dangerous use. According to Allende, Einstein discussed these fears with his friend Bertrand Russell, and Lord Russell concurred.

Since Allende himself is not willing to divulge his source of information on this aspect of our topic, we are left with the alternatives of either pursuing the truth on our own, or accepting his word on the matter. Admittedly, trying to substantiate a statement such as this is no easy task even though the people involved are famous, but a reasonably thorough attempt to look into it was made and resulted in several interesting bits of information. Among them the following:

1. Dr. Einstein did indeed complete a version of his "Unified Field Theory for Gravitation and Electricity" in the period 1925–27. The results, published in German, appeared in Prussian scientific journals for 1925 and 1927. Allende is also correct in stating that this work was "withdrawn" as incomplete, although no published reason is given save that Dr. Einstein was not satisfied with it as it stood. Significantly, the theory did not reappear until 1940, at a point *after* the basically pacifistic Dr. Einstein had already become convinced that the Nazi menace must be destroyed at all costs and that warfare was morally justifiable under such circumstances. Also, evidence which we will deal with later strongly indicates that 1940 was the year that the Navy first began working on the project which developed into the Philadelphia Experiment.

2. Einstein was indeed friendly with Bertrand Russell, especially in the period after World War II, and frequently discussed paci-

fism with him. Both men had a horror of mankind's disturbing tendency to use scientific developments for purposes of self-destruction, and both devoted a substantial portion of their efforts and personal finances to the cause of world peace.

Allende wrote that Lord Russell considered Einstein's Unified Field Theory complete, but felt that "Man is not ready for it and shan't be until after World War III," and that Einstein's judgment of man's "progress compared to the growth of [his]...character was enough to horrify him." These statements are most interesting in light of the actual facts concerning these two men and their attitudes toward humanity and world peace. Banesh Hoffmann and Helen Dukas (who was Einstein's personal secretary), for example, report the following in their book *Albert Einstein, Creator and Rebel* (New York: The Viking Press, 1972):

...when the bomb was exploded over Hiroshima his worst fears were realized. His horror of the bomb, whether in dictatorial or democratic hands, weighed heavily on his conscience. Not because he had written urgently to Roosevelt in 1939, when he feared the Nazis would develop the weapon first and then control the world. Not because, in all innocence, he had propounded the formula $E = mc^2$ in 1907. Not for these reasons, but because...he felt a moral obligation to use his influence to the utmost to try to save mankind from horrors that, despite Hiroshima and Nagasaki, it did not yet comprehend.

Certainly it is not too far out of line to presume that he had the same feelings about the even more horrifying potentials of his Unified Field Theory.

As for Lord Russell, at least one of his biographers (Ronald Clark) reports that he somehow was permitted to see a highly secret British intelligence report on "new weapon developments" immediately following World War II, and that what he read shocked him so deeply that he was moved to press for a "manifesto for world peace" which he hoped would eventually be signed by every prominent thinker on earth. Einstein agreed to sign such a document just before he died.

Dr. J. Robert Oppenheimer, often referred to as the "godfather" of the atomic bomb had, like Einstein, considerable doubts about its morality, although it is unknown whether he felt impelled at any time to cease or destroy research that seemed to go too far. But one recalls his thoughts as he saw the first bomb exploded at Alamogordo in 1945. A passage from the ancient Hindu epic, the Mahabharata, immediately came to his mind.

> If the radiance of a thousand suns
> were to burst at once in the sky,
> That would be like the splendor

of the Mighty One...
I am become Death
The destroyer of worlds.

The notion that Einstein destroyed papers
before his death is also an interesting one, although never substantiated beyond the rumor
stage. One such story has it that some months
before his death Einstein had burned papers
relating to some of his more advanced theories
on the grounds that the world wasn't ready for
such things and would be better off without
them. Presumably these had something to do
with his conclusions regarding his Unified Field
Theory and the possible practical applications
of the same.

3. In 1943, during the time Allende states he
witnessed a manifestation of the Philadelphia
Experiment at sea, Dr. Einstein was employed
by the U.S. Navy as a scientific consultant, ostensibly for the Bureau of Ordinance. Records
of the Office of the General Services Administration in St. Louis show that Einstein was employed "intermittently in a Special Services
Contract of the Department of the Navy, Washington, D.C. as a *scientist* from May 31, 1943,
to June 30, 1944."

Einstein's own comments on this association
are sketchy, but interesting. In July 1943,
Clark quotes him as having written to his friend
Gustav Buckley that "so long as the war lasts
and I work for the Navy, I do not wish to begin
anything else." In August he again wrote to

Albert Einstein conferring with naval officers in his study at Princeton, New Jersey, July 24, 1943. (*National Archives*)

Buckley, saying he had developed "closer relations to the Navy Office of Scientific Research and Development in Washington." That same month, Dr. Vannevar Bush appointed him to "a committee where it seemed ... his particular skills would be most likely to be of service." Neither the exact nature of this "committee" nor the skills involved have ever been disclosed.

An inquiry to Dr. Otto Nathan, Einstein's financial adviser and executor of his estate in New York, concerning the extent of Dr. Einstein's involvement with the Navy produced a confusing response. "Einstein," he said, "... became a consultant to the Navy's Bureau of Ordinance [*sic*] in 1943 and, as far as we know, terminated his work with the Navy quite some time before the end of the War.... In case you are interested in more details we suggest you communicate with the Navy Department in Washington. Since Einstein's work was in no way secret they may be in a position to give you more information about the consulting work he did which we were unable to obtain [from them] when we prepared [our] volume for publication." If the reader is confused, he should be; for the very same sentence that tells us that Einstein's work for the Navy was "in no way secret" goes right on to explain that the Navy wasn't willing to talk about it!

4. What of the Unified Field Theory itself? It is virtually impossible to discuss it in nontechnical terms, but the general thrust of the theory is to explain mathematically by means

of a single set of equations (presumably from which a scientific law could be derived) the interrelationships among the three basic universal forces: electromagnetic, gravitational and nuclear. (Interestingly, in 1974 the simultaneous discovery in New York and California of two elementary particles of matter, known as J or psi particles, seems to suggest that there may be a fourth "weak" universal force which could be related to gravity in the same way that electricity is related to magnetism. Whether such a "field" would be interdimensional or "time-related" is not yet known.) Anyhow, presuming that such a theory could be completely developed, it would also have to incorporate light, radio waves, pure magnetism, X-rays, and even matter itself into its final equations. The enormous complexity of such a problem can be envisioned when one considers that Einstein spent the greater part of his life in pursuit of just such a goal, and, in later years, frequently was heard to complain that he did not have enough mathematics to complete the task.

As early as 1916, Einstein was busy exploring the possibility that gravity is not really a "force" at all, but rather one of the observable properties of "space-time" itself—the force that underlies and governs all of the other forces in what we consider to be "our" universe. Going one step further, he speculated that what we know as substance, or "matter," is in reality only a local phenomenon exhibited by areas of extreme field-energy concentration. In more simple terms, he chose to view *matter* as a *product of energy* rather than the reverse, and in so doing dared to reject the long-standing concept that the two are separate entities that exist side by side.

During the next thirty-nine years, until his death in 1955 at the age of seventy-six, he continued to refine this concept, occasionally altering his point of view, but never altering his basic premise that gravity could be mathematically proved to be directly related to other forms of energy—principally electromagnetism. Taking this concept to its logical conclusion (with apologies for the gross oversimplification necessary to make a point): Since it is demonstrable that electricity can be readily obtained from a magnetic field (the principle of the common electrical generator) and that magnetic fields can be easily derived from electrical ones (industrial electromagnets, for example), then it logically follows that if gravity is related to these it should be possible to obtain (or nullify) a gravitational field through some sort of interaction with either one, or both, of the other two.

Virtually every advantage of our twentieth-century way of life, from automobiles to toasters and microwave ovens, is based on our having learned, in the final years of the last century, how to make the interactions between electricity and magnetism work for us as a source of power. Up to this point, however, we are told that any demonstrable relationship of the third side of this triangle to the other two has largely eluded us.

Even more than twenty years after Einstein's death, much of his life's work still remains largely incomprehensible to even the most brilliant scholars. In general, orthodox science in the 1970s does tend to recognize a loose linking or "coupling effect" of some sort between electromagnetic and gravitational forces, but few scientists have speculated that this coupling effect is at all applicable. Officially that is the case, although one suspects that some significant advances in this area still remain hidden under the awesome phrase "Top Secret." (The authors, for example, have seen a most interesting study dealing with the possibility of generating "gravitational rays" using laser technology and using these virtually undetectable rays to transmit intelligence from one point to another.)

Einstein viewed the universe as an orderly and coherent creation. He was unable to believe that the physical laws governing God's perfection could possibly be a chaotic collection of equations bearing only the remotest of relationships to one another. "God," he said, "does not play dice with the world." Hence, the forces of the universe must represent an orderly, coherent whole which, if the proper techniques are employed, can be portrayed to a greater or lesser extent in mathematical terms.

Interestingly enough, Einstein stood nearly alone in the pursuit of this goal. Today most scientists are far too concerned with the press of experimental research to bother with the rigorous mental gymnastics necessary to explore the underlying fundamentals of the Unified Field Theory—not to mention the fact that the task is appallingly difficult and time-consuming and frequently not very rewarding. It is, alas, one of the hard realities of scientific life that research resulting in usable "hardware" tends to be more profitable than research which leads only to theories. Even further complicating the task is the fact that many scientists today feel that Einstein was pursuing a nonexistent goal in trying to obtain order from chaos. (Indeed, Wolfgang Pauli, a physicist who gave up working in Unified Field physics, is said to have quipped as a reflection of his disgust: "What God has put asunder, let no man put together.")

Exactly how successful Einstein was may never be known, since so few are able to comprehend exactly what he was up to when he died. If the Philadelphia Experiment did manage to confirm some of his theoretical positions, that knowledge has been so suppressed that even today his concepts of a Unified Field Theory are regarded more as goal than as actual theory. This in spite of the fact that less than two years before his death Einstein announced what he referred to as "highly convincing" results in his quest to find a mathematical proof of the connection between the forces of electromagnetism and gravity. Keeping in mind

Allende's statements concerning the completeness of Einstein's Unified Field Theory in 1925, it is significant to note that this last theory was really a very close cousin to that earlier version which Allende says was "withdrawn" for reasons of "humantics."

The thrust of this theory was a string of sixteen incredibly complex quantities (represented by an advanced type of mathematical shorthand known as tensor equations), ten combinations of which represented gravitation and the remaining six electromagnetism. According to those who have studied the revised version, there is no satisfactory way to explain this final theory in simple terms, since it is so intensely mathematical in its concepts. And, as if to add to the problem, Einstein himself stated that his equations were not necessarily in their final form, thus making the task of trying to reconstruct his efforts doubly difficult. One thing that does emerge, interestingly, is the concept that a pure gravitational field can exist without an electromagnetic field, but a pure electromagnetic field cannot exist without an accompanying gravitational field.

Little of any consequence has been added to Einstein's calculations since his final revision in 1953; and indeed it may be a good many more years before anything is added, since there is no easy way of solving the equations involved. Experimental work which bypasses equations in favor of results is either kept secret or ignored, and computers are of only limited help, since they are not designed to solve problems of such an abstract nature.

Possibly of interest at this point, however, is a tiny filler item from an April 1956 edition of *The New York Times* which reported that a Dr. Parvis Marat, physicist from the University of Maryland, had "partly confirmed the late Dr. Albert Einstein's famous Unified Field Theory," and that "Einstein's newest and most radical theory had come through one stage of critical tests with flying colors." The nature of those "critical tests" remained undisclosed.

But however interesting theoretical findings may be, it takes demonstrated practical results to really raise eyebrows. Were these results obtained and the accompanying eyebrows raised as far back as 1943 when the Navy tried to utilize some of the principles we have just discussed to create and perhaps to teleport the invisible ship Allende claimed to have witnessed? Did the experiment somehow go wrong and produce unexpectedly disastrous results—perhaps results of a type which, if we can believe the statements made to Davis and Huse in Colorado, may even have led to contact with aliens from another world?

Was Allende correct when he hinted in the closing words of his final letter to Dr. Jessup that the results of the Navy's secret experimentation might have something to do with UFO propulsion? Or was it all merely a "mirage" of some sort—perhaps one of those elusive "ghost" ships that seem to appear and disappear at will out of the ocean mists?

Our search for the answer takes us next to the National Archives in Washington, D.C.

CHAPTER 8

The Elusive Archives

One of the biggest problems that can confront a researcher is that of trying to verify information. If Allende's strange tale is true—if indeed the DE 173 did become invisible as he says it did, and if the experiment was witnessed from the deck of the *S.S. Andrew Furuseth*—then, failing a knowledge of the actual name of the project, perhaps one of the best ways to try to learn more about it is to check out the available government archives on the ships involved. Once again, however, what began as an honest effort to discredit the tale ended with the uncovering of facts which seem to do just the opposite.

To begin with, there appear to be not one but two *S.S. Andrew Furuseths*. The first, an ore carrier in the Pacific which is apparently still operating, can be effectively eliminated from our investigation, since it was not in service until after World War II. The second, a Liberty

Ship, checks out remarkably well with Allende's information.

The name *Andrew Furuseth* was actually suggested to the United States Maritime Commission as a name for a ship by the Seamen's Union of the Pacific in July 1942 as an appropriate honor to that organization's founder and longtime president. The ship itself was launched in October of that same year as Hull No. 491 at Yard No. 1 of the Permanente Metals Division of Kaiser Industries at Richmond, Calif. True to Allende's statement to Jessup, shortly after launch the ship was leased to the Matson Navigation Company of San Francisco—a company which was to operate her for the next four years. On October 19 she steamed from that city bound for a five-month tour of duty that was to take her well into the Pacific war zone. March 1943, however, found her at the Pacific Island of Luganville facing orders to transfer to the Atlantic as a much-needed replacement on the dangerous supply run to North Africa. Matson records indicate that the long trip to and through the Canal was begun on March 14, and that the *Furuseth* finally arrived in New York Harbor on May 6. Twenty-two days later, after a brief overhaul, the *Furuseth* departed New York in convoy bound for Oran, Algeria, where she arrived safely on June 17.

After calling at Mostaganem and Gibraltar, she again arrived in New York on July 23 for another three-week stay. On August 13, 1943, the *Furuseth* left New York to begin a trip down the coast to the Norfolk–Newport News port facilities to load for another trip across the Atlantic. It is here that we begin to become interested in her, for one of the newly assigned members of the deck crew on this voyage is a young man fresh out of seamen's school who signs on under the name Carl M. Allen. Of particular interest is the fact that rather than sailing along with the *Furuseth* on the short voyage down the coast, he receives permission to join the ship at Norfolk, and so makes the journey overland—a trip which results in his stopping in Philadelphia for an overnight on the way. He arrived in the Norfolk Harbor vicinity on the morning of the 16th in time to join the *Furuseth* before she left Newport News at 10:18 A.M. on her third voyage as part of a convoy bound for Casablanca.

October 4 finds the *Furuseth* again docking at Newport News for repairs and reloading—a process which takes until October 25. On that date she again departs for North Africa (this time for Oran), and again a Carl M. Allen is listed among the crew. The ship reached port safely on November 12, and did not return to an American port again until January 17, 1944. A few days later, the crew member calling himself Carl M. Allen left the *Furuseth* for the final time. He was eventually to transfer to the deck crew of another ship—the *S.S. Newton D. Baker.*

As for the DE 173, better known as the destroyer escort U.S.S. *Eldridge,* the *official* rec-

Federal Ship Basin and Drydock at Port Newark, New Jersey, where the U.S.S. *Eldridge* (DE 173) was built. This photo was kept under classification by the Navy for twenty-two years. (*National Archives*)

The U.S.S. *Eldridge* (DE 173) on September 12, 1943. (*National Archives*)

ords indicate that the ship had a rather uneventful history. Information in these records indicates that the *Eldridge* was laid down on February 22, 1943, at Federal Shipbuilding and Drydocks, Newark, N.J., and that she had a length of 306 feet and a displacement of 1,240 tons standard and 1,520 tons full load. Some five months later, on July 25, we are told that the ship was launched. The official commissioning ceremony took place on August 27 at the New York Navy Yard, at which time Lieutenant Charles R. Hamilton, USNR, took command.

Quoting from the ship's history as recorded by the Department of the Navy:

Wasting no time in getting to the task in hand, *U.S.S. Eldridge* during the month of September, combined escort duty with shakedown operations in the Bermuda, British West Indies, area. She continued in this duty until December 28, when she took time out for a three day training period in the vicinity of Block Island. From the Block Island area she proceeded down the coast to Hampton Roads, Virginia, there to await her first overseas escort assignment. After brief escort and patrol missions which took her into the Chesapeake Bay during the first week of January 1944, the ship headed out across the Atlantic as one of the escort units to a large convoy of merchant ships. . . .

Between January 4, 1944 and May 9, 1945,

Eldridge sailed on the vital task of escorting to the Mediterranean men and materials to support allied operations in North Africa and on into Southern Europe. She made nine voyages to deliver convoys safely to Casablanca, Bizerte and Oran.

Following service in the Atlantic, the *Eldridge* was transferred to the Pacific, where she remained until the end of the war. Upon returning to New York, she was placed out of commission on June 17, 1946, and remained in reserve until January 15, 1951, when she was sold under the Mutual Defense Assistance Program to Greece. There she was renamed the *Léon* ("Lion"), and is apparently still in service.

All of which sounds so officially normal that one would hardly be motivated to look any further into the matter if it were not for Allende's story about the ship. However, upon subsequent examination in light of Allende's story, this neat, *official* history of the *Eldridge* shows signs of considerable patching and doctoring.

To begin at the beginning: If the *Eldridge* and the S.S. *Furuseth* could be shown to have been in the same place on even as little as one single date during the period that Carl M. Allen was a crew member of the *Furuseth,* then at the very least an air of possibility is added to his story. On the other hand, if no such similarity of positions can be shown, then Allende's tale is seriously (and perhaps fatally) damaged. The first hint that all was not as it should be came when Moore attempted to check this aspect of the mystery by trying to obtain copies of the logbooks of the two ships in question. The result of such a request was the surprising discovery that (1) the deck logs of the *Eldridge* for the period from date of commission (August 27, 1943) through December 1, 1943, were "missing and therefore unavailable"; and (2) the logbooks of the *Furuseth* had been "destroyed by executive order" and thus no longer exist.

Since the only period of time in the history of these two ships which is of any interest to this investigation is that time during which Allende served aboard the S.S. *Furuseth*—i.e., from about August 13, 1943, through about January 30, 1944—the next step was to attempt to arrive at certain sketchy and purely tentative conclusions by falling back upon an examination of information available and already in hand. Such an examination seemed to indicate the following.

According to records still in possession of the Matson Navigation Company, the *Furuseth* made two complete voyages to North Africa in this time period: the first beginning on August 13, 1943, when the *Furuseth* left New York to sail down the coast to Norfolk and from there on to North Africa; and the second beginning on October 25, 1943, when she sailed from Lynhaven Roads, Virginia (Norfolk area), bound for Oran, Algeria. The first voyage did not begin for Allende until August 16, when he joined ship at Norfolk after spending a weekend in

Philadelphia. The second ended with the arrival of the *Furuseth* at Hampton Roads on January 17, 1944, and his leaving the ship a few days later.

According to the Navy Department's official history of the *Eldridge,* that ship was launched July 25, 1943, at Newark, New Jersey, and commissioned August 27, 1943, at New York Navy Yard. Her shakedown cruise began early in September, took place in the area of Bermuda, British West Indies, and lasted until December 28. These same records indicate that her first overseas voyage began on January 4, 1944, and ended on February 15 with her arrival in New York Harbor.

If we are to base our conclusions on this material, then the two ships do not appear to have been in each other's vicinity at all during this time period. But is this information reliable? The mysterious unavailability of the ships' logbooks casts certain doubts upon it, but is hardly enough to seriously discredit the records. The mystery was no nearer a solution than it was before.

The first missing piece that fitted into the puzzle came quite unexpectedly with the uncovering of a previously classified bit of information about the *Eldridge* which seemed to discredit the official histories completely. The document in question was a report on Antisubmarine Action by Surface Ship filed by the commander of the *Eldridge* on December 14, 1943, in accordance with fleet regulations, and concerned an action which took place on November 20 in the North Atlantic. According to official histories, the *Eldridge* was operating on a shakedown cruise in the vicinity of Bermuda from early September until late December 1943, and her first overseas voyage began on January 4, 1944. According to the action report filed by ship's commander, Lieutenant C.R. Hamilton, the *Eldridge* dropped seven depth charges against a suspected enemy submarine shortly after 1:30 P.M. local time on the afternoon of November 20, 1943, while steaming *westward* (towards the United States) in escort of convoy UGS 23. The position of the *Eldridge* as listed in the report was latitude 34°03' north and longitude 08°57' west—a position which places the ship barely 200 miles off the coast of Casablanca, North Africa, and some 3,000 miles from Bermuda!

Then, a second piece of information began to complete the picture: While the missing deck logs of the *Eldridge* had still not turned up, the engineer's log had. While not containing much information related to the search, it did contain a record of the ship's positions for the dates in question, which were missing from the deck-log file. This and other documentation which came to light at about the same time showed that the *Eldridge* had indeed steamed out of port (Brooklyn) on November 2 to round up stragglers from convoy GUS 22 which had been knocked out of line by a late-season hurricane blowing up from the south in the last days of October. This was a valuable piece of information indeed, since the convoy in question was none other than the *S.S. Furuseth*'s convoy, which had left Norfolk–Lynhaven Roads on October 25! And more important, the *Furuseth*'s steaming along in the last rank of the convoy, is almost certain to have caught sight of the DE 173 as it mothered stragglers back into line. Furthermore, the *Eldridge*'s reported position off Casablanca on November 20 seems to indicate that the *Eldridge* accompanied the *Furuseth* and her GUS 22 convoy all the way to North Africa (the convoy arrived there on November 12, remember), and was on her return trip home escorting GUS 23 when she encountered the submarine mentioned in the action report. Were it not for the discovery of this action report, which had been kept classified by the Navy for some thirty-four years, none of this would ever have come to light. But now, with the discovery of one glaring "error" in the *official* histories, the question had rapidly become: Could there be others?

Clearly the *Furuseth* and the *Eldridge* were within sight of each other in a convoy operation on the way to Africa; but would it be logical for the Navy, or Navy scientists, to risk attempting such a dangerous, daring, and obviously Top Secret experiment as electromagnetic invisibility under such circumstances and in full view of an entire convoy? It certainly doesn't seem likely. And then too, Allende seems to indicate explicitly that the experiments took place at dockside in Philadelphia and "at sea"—presum-

ably off the coast of the mainland. His dates—
the latter part of October—coincide with the
convoy operation, but the other circumstances
do not; especially since the *Eldridge* steamed
out of Brooklyn, not Philadelphia, to join GUS
22. In fact, nowhere in the ship's records for the
period in question does it indicate that the *Eldridge* was ever even in or near the Philadelphia area—except during the time she was under construction at Newark. Note also that
Allende tells Jessup that he read of the effects
of the experiment on some of the ship's crew in
an article which he says appeared in a Philadelphia newspaper. It does not appear that Allende (or Allen) was in Philadelphia in October
1943 either; but he *was* there in August—coincidentally at about the same time that the
Eldridge was supposedly at Newark awaiting
orders to transfer to New York for commissioning ceremonies. Yet in his letter he says he feels
that the article he read appeared in a fall or
winter edition of the paper rather than a summer issue. If we can chalk this final item up to
the failings of human memory, then we might
be able to make something of the remainder.

It was while pondering this problem that the
final clues, important ones which appear to cast
doubt on the official records, came to light.
About this time Moore received a letter from a
correspondent who was a former ship commander during the war, and who wrote that he
was virtually certain he recalled the *Eldridge*
putting in to Bermuda immediately following

the *first* hurricane of the season in 1943—a date which he feels would have to have been in late July or early August of that year! The ship, he said, anchored near his own for a brief period of time and then put out to sea again almost immediately. The reason he recalled the incident, he said, was that the ship was flying no signal flags and made no effort to exchange greetings with his own.

Strange behavior indeed; but even stranger is the fact that if this ship was the *Eldridge,* then its appearance in Bermuda took place only days after its launch at Newark—at a time when the final phases of the ship's construction would normally not yet be complete, and fully a month before the ship was even assigned a crew!

The only possible explanation for such an occurrence is that either the officer in question was mistaken, or the *Eldridge* was launched at Newark before July 25. Certainly the records of the American Navy make no such indications, but what about the Greeks? Here came yet another surprise, for according to the Greek records on the *Eldridge* (which must, of course, have been obtained from the Americans) that ship was launched not on July 25, but on *June* 25—a full thirty days earlier! Not only that, but the Greek records show that the *Eldridge,* when transferred to the Greek navy in 1951, was rated at 1,240 tons displacement standard and *1,900* full load, a discrepancy of some 660 tons. According to one former Navy man, the only

way for a ship to gain 660 tons of buoyancy is
for something of that weight to have been re-
moved from that ship before the time of its sale
to the Greeks. Electronics equipment, perhaps?

The whole story now begins to come together.
The *Eldridge* was launched on June 25 rather
than July 25; she was ported in the Newark–
Philadelphia area until the time of her transfer
in August for the official commissioning; she
was at sea at least as far as Bermuda in late
July or the first few days of August; and her
official history for the period up to January 4,
1944, is almost certainly false!

Armed with this evidence, Moore confronted
a contact who up to this point had been helpful
in small things, but who was suspected of knowing more than he was telling. This individual,
who must of necessity go nameless, had been
employed as a scientist in the Navy's radar program during the war in a capacity which, had
such a project as the Philadelphia Experiment
ever occurred, almost certainly would have put
him into contact with it. At Moore's urging, and
confronted with the evidence above, he finally
agreed to speak with the provision that he be
guaranteed complete anonymity. He was, and
his story follows:

Question: *Commander, can you describe
the procedure which was followed in obtaining an experimental ship for this project?*

You must remember that in '43 ships were
hard to come by for experimental purposes.

Once the commissioning took place, a ship immediately became part of some admiral's war plans, and to shake it loose from those plans for experimental work was wellnigh impossible. Consequently the easiest, and in fact virtually the only, way to get a ship for use in such a project was to divert one into experimental work for a short period of time in between launch and commissioning. Such a process was seldom easy and generally required a certain amount of maneuverings and manipulatings in high places, but it could be, and in fact was done—provided, of course, that the scientists could convince the necessary brass that the project in question was of sufficient enough promise and importance to warrant it. Nonetheless, it was generally much easier to get a handle on a ship which was not yet assigned and still in the construction phases. There were generally fewer people here that had to be maneuvered around.

Question: *Considering that the Manhattan Project was beginning to show marked progress by mid-1943 and was beginning to siphon off a large chunk of the funds available for military research, wasn't 1943 a rather crucial year for a great many of the other Top Secret defense-oriented projects which were then also in progress?*

From about 1943 on, attitudes about various experimental projects and ideas in the works began to take on a marked change. By this time there were those who began to see the end of the war in sight, and so the question for all work in progress became, "Can you get it done before the end of the war so some use can be made of it?" Those teams who weren't sure of certain projects were urged to do some quick experimentation or testing so that they could be more certain of possible uses. If these couldn't be accomplished quickly or if results were still clouded, then a directive inevitably came down to the team in question to the effect that "your time is perhaps more valuable on more important things." Projects which had little hope of producing some immediately useful results were almost certain to be shelved "for the duration."

Question: *Doesn't the very fact that a ship was obtained tend to indicate something about the importance with which this project was regarded by the military-scientific establishment?*

I am not what you would call overly familiar with the project you have in question, but I believe what occurred was that someone said to the Navy [scientific] people something to the effect that "if you can do a test this year ('43), we're interested and we'll back you. If not, stop. Whether we will go on or not with this will depend entirely on the results of the tests you do. If immediate results are not forthcoming, shelve it until the end of the war and we'll take another look at it then."

Question: *Concerning the actual project itself, can you recall anything about how it began, who was behind it, or what they were ultimately hoping to accomplish?*

Where such a project came from or how it initially got started, I have no idea. As I say, my immediate knowledge of it was largely peripheral. I believe they did succeed in getting a ship out of Philadelphia or Newark for a limited time, probably not more than two or three weeks, and I think I heard they did some testing both along the river [the Delaware] and off the coast, especially with regard to the effects of a strong magnetic force field on radar detection apparatus. I can't tell you much else about it or about what the results ultimately were because I don't know. My guess, and I emphasize *guess,* would be that every kind of receiving equipment possible was put aboard other vessels and along the shoreline to check on what would happen on the "other side" when both radio and low- and high-frequency radar were projected through the field. Undoubtedly observations would have also been made as to any effects that field might have had on light in the visual range. In any event, I do know that there was a great deal of work being done on total absorption as well as refraction, and this would certainly seem to tie in with such an experiment as this.

One thing I can tell you: It is highly unlikely that any experimental work of such a nature as this would have taken place aboard a ship after it was commissioned and had a crew. Such a thing just wouldn't have been done—especially not at sea while on convoy duty. Absolutely no one doing research of this type in '43 would have dared to risk placing several hundred tons of valuable electronics equipment at the mercy of some German submarine commander in the middle of the Atlantic.

All of this is very valuable testimony indeed, since it tells us almost exactly when the Philadelphia Experiment took place, and in fact even seems to indicate that at least part of it took place in or around the Philadelphia-Newark dockyard facilities. If indeed the two-to-three-week period of availability for research purposes is correct, and if the Greek records on the *Eldridge* are correct concerning a June 25 launch date (as we must assume they are), then, allowing for several weeks to complete final construction phases after launch, it appears that the Philadelphia Experiment took place sometime between July 20 and August 20, 1943. This not only explains how the former Navy commander mentioned above happened to see the *Eldridge* in Bermuda in the last days of July (where she may have been forced to go because of the hurricane), but it also explains how Carlos Allende, who was in Philadelphia during the weekend of August 13–15, happened to catch an item about it in a Philadelphia or Philadelphia-area newspaper. The experiments would have to have been in their final phases at that time, and conceivably the skeleton crew which would have been used to man the ship during research operations might have been granted a shore leave on one of those evenings. If so, then the date of the barroom brawl that Allende mentions was either Friday evening, August 13, or Saturday evening, August 14.

According to records, the *Eldridge* left Newark bound for Brooklyn on Tuesday, August 17, and arrived there to await commissioning on Wednesday, August 18. The *Furuseth,* which had left the Norfolk Harbor area with Allende on board on Monday, August 16, and was proceeding in convoy up the coast on the 17th prior to turning eastward toward Africa, could easily have encountered the *Eldridge* as it emerged from Delaware Bay on the morning of the 17th bound for Brooklyn. Any such encounter would most likely have been brief, because of the *Eldridge*'s greater speed and different destination, but if final experiments were still going on at this time, then it is entirely possible that Allende's chance encounter with them took place on this date rather than during the period of his second encounter with the *Eldridge,* which event took place, as we have already described, in November.

Did it really happen? At this point the affirmative evidence seems to be just tipping the scales toward credibility.

CHAPTER 9

The Unexpected
Key

Having apparently exhausted the information available in the existing ship records, we must now turn our attention to the one item of the Allende letters that has stopped so many researchers cold in their tracks and that, if ever substantiated, could provide the key to the entire mystery. The reader will recall that early in his second letter to Dr. Jessup, Allende made an assertion to the effect that not only was Einstein's Unified Field Theory completed between 1925 and 1927, but the entire theory was subjected by the Navy to a "complete (group math) recheck ... with a view to any and every possible quick use of it ... in a very short time." If Allende is to be believed, then it was the results of this mathematical process which supposedly provided the theoretical basis for what was eventually to become the Philadelphia Experiment.

The possible key provided here is that Allende takes pains to provide Dr. Jessup with the name of the scientist allegedly in charge of this "recheck." This man is identified as Dr. Franklin Reno, a man to whom Allende refers quite offhandedly as "my friend."

Obviously if this Dr. Reno could be found, and if he could be convinced to add his testimony to the research which has already been done, then a great portion of the mystery could conceivably be revealed. The problem up to this point has been that although many have tried, no one has ever been able to crack this part of the story—a fact that has led more than one researcher to conclude that since this mysterious individual could not be produced, then the entire matter must be considered nothing more than a hoax.

Now, after several years of persistent research into this aspect of the affair, the authors at last feel that the riddle surrounding the identity of the elusive Dr. Reno has been solved! And with it comes a fantastic tale which seems to provide for the first time some substantial insights into the mystery which for so long has enshrouded the so-called Philadelphia Experiment. Now, for the first time ever in print, we have a sequence of events which appear to have been indisputable forerunners of that Top Secret project which may well have developed into a full-scale ship experiment of the sort described by Allende in his angry letters to Dr. Jessup! The story itself is almost as odd as the Allende letters.

The substance of that story is that the man referred to by Allende as Dr. Franklin Reno was not only a very real person but, before his death only a little more than a year before this writing, he personally verified to Moore the substantial truth of Allende's statements concerning the beginnings of the project which came to be known as the Philadelphia Experiment.

The reason why earlier researchers were completely unsuccessful in their efforts to find this Franklin Reno is easily explained by the simple fact that they were looking for a man whose name was not Franklin Reno, although a clue to the name and the whereabouts of the man was on a road map of the state of Pennsylvania!

In the oil-producing region of northwestern Pennsylvania, along U.S. Route 62 not far from Oil City, lies the city of Franklin, Pennsylvania—a peaceful little trading center of about 8,000 population and the county seat of Venango County. Five miles to the east, still on the same road and about midway between Franklin and Oil City, lies the village of Reno, home of a large refinery of the Wolf's Head Oil Company. Just outside this same Oil City, on the westbound side of Route 62, stood, until a few years ago, the road sign that explains why so many diligent researchers have been so consistently unsuccessful in their efforts to identify Allende's mysterious "friend." Printed on this sign were the words

| FRANKLIN | 8 |
| RENO | 3 |

—the same words which inspired a very real scientist over thirty years ago to create a very effective pseudonym.

But if "Franklin Reno" is nothing more than a pseudonym, then the questions now become: (1) Who is this real person? (2) What is (or was) his connection with Carlos Miguel Allende? (3) What, if anything, can he add to the story?

Unfortunately the matter is so sensitive that these questions cannot be entirely answered even yet for reasons which the reader will come to understand as the story progresses. For even though the man Allende knew as Dr. Reno has since died, we have been enjoined to be discreet by those still living who are very interested in maintaining the status quo. Consequently, we have chosen to refer to this individual as Dr. Rinehart, the name given to him in a fictionalized version of the Philadelphia Experiment published recently, representing yet another indication of increasing public interest and awareness in the "impossible" experiment.

What can be told, then, while still safely concealing as much of Dr. Rinehart's identity as possible, is that he was born within a few years of Morris Jessup, but in a quite different part of the country. After serving brilliantly in a well-known civilian scientific establishment for a number of years while at the same time successfully completing the requirements for his Ph.D. degree, he was forced during the depression years of the 1930s, like so many other scientists including Dr. Jessup, to enter the employ of America's governmental military-scientific establishment. It was here, over the course of the next decade, that he worked himself up to a position as a department head in a well-known research installation; and it was in that capacity that he came into contact with the early phases of the project which all indications point to as the beginnings of the Philadelphia Experiment.

Discovering the real identity of this individual, however, proved to be a small problem compared to the task of finding him after some twenty-five years and then winning enough of his confidence to convince him that his story should be told. A quarter-century is time enough for a great many changes—especially when someone chooses to use that time to isolate himself from his fellow man.

So it was with Dr. Rinehart, who, when he began to suspect he knew too much for his own good (and perhaps for his survival), chose to hide himself away from the segments of society that seemed to threaten him the most. Those years had seen him abandon a brilliant and promising scientific career to install himself in a neat little bungalow nestled between the hills half a continent away and content himself with living the life of a hermit—venturing out only occasionally for supplies, or even more occasionally to visit an old friend or former colleague.

Moore and Rinehart corresponded for nearly a year before any mention was made of the possibility of doing a personal interview, and it was to be several months more before the necessary arrangements could be worked out.

Moore's account of the interview follows:

It was late on a hot July afternoon when I parked my car at a discreet distance and walked slowly the rest of the way to his house, trying hard not to attract any undue attention.

I recall a foreboding that perhaps my trip would prove useless after all; for aside from a disused sprinkler resting forlornly on the scraggly brown uncut lawn, the place had a stark, almost deserted look about it. Why, I wondered, would anyone keep a house so tightly closed up and curtained in such heat?

A striped cat lounging lazily on the railing raised an inquisitive eyelid as I stepped onto the porch, but didn't bother moving. I knocked at the door and somewhere inside, something stirred. Presently the curtain was brushed slightly aside and a pair of spectacled, rabbit-like eyes peered at me suspiciously. A pause, the click of a lock, and the door swung open to reveal a spindly, white-haired, but sharp-eyed old gentleman trying somehow to force a smile through his uncertain expression.

"Hello," I said, taking advantage of the awkward pause to introduce myself. "I spoke with you this morning on the phone."

"Yes," came the slow but deliberate reply. "I know. I've been expecting you. Won't you come in?"

The house was small but comfortable enough, and unexpectedly cool—a welcome change from the afternoon heat. A small, ancient aluminum fan was purring from its place on the sitting-room floor, sending a thin stream of welcome breeze back and forth across the otherwise silent room.

"Seat?" said the old gentleman, indicating an aging and somewhat sway-backed sofa in the front corner of the room.

"Thanks," I replied, looking around. "You certainly seem to have found a comfortable enough means of keeping out of the world's way up here. I can't imagine you get very many visitors."

"If I wanted visitors, I wouldn't be here," he replied, fixing me with a slightly suspicious eye. "Actually, I live comfortably enough, all things considered. No one bothers me much, and I don't bother anyone else either. I try to keep it that way."

Speaking guardedly at first, Dr. Rinehart slowly warmed to his topic.

"They still watch over me, you know. In fact, it's actually come to the point where I try to avoid going certain places in the town because of the sudden interest my appearance there seems to create—especially around certain buildings down at the university. I used to like to pay an occasional visit to that place, but the security guards seem somehow keyed to react to my presence there, so I don't go much any more. Same thing happens when I show an interest in purchasing travel tickets. Soon as I give my name, the security people perk up. I tried it once just to see if it wasn't my imagination. It wasn't.

"So you came all this way just to discover what I can tell you about that ship experiment, did you? You know, I've done a good deal of thinking about that since you first made contact. I'm an old man now, and that was a long time ago. Memory is a bit hazy on some of the details, but if you're willing to do a lot of listening, I'm willing to take a chance on you and let a few cats out of the bag—provided, of course, that you haven't forgotten your promise regarding my anonymity. That above all else is important. In fact, you might say it's become the key word of my life style of late."

"I remember the promise," I said, attempting a smile, "and when it comes to an opportunity like this one, I can also be a very good listener." I waited.

He stared at me a moment as if trying to clear away the last lingering doubts about what he was about to say. Then, settling back in his chair, he began to unravel one of the strangest tales I have ever heard.

"You know, of course," he began, "that an

experiment first begins as an idea, then a thought proposition (tested by calculation or the like), then a project, and finally an experiment, or experiments, in the usual sense. The persons initially concerned with this one were very few. Most had somewhat varied immediacies to contend against."

Again a pause, presumably for a moment's reflection on just how he should proceed. When he resumed speaking, the words came slowly and seemed to have been chosen carefully.

"The Unified Field Theory," he resumed, "has remained an incomplete structure—even today. No one can properly claim to have made a complete 'recheck' of 'that theory' in my view. Of course, there have been contributions toward the goal, and several papers with the title (the German is *Einheitliche-Feld Theorie*), but the substance of those papers are not 'complete' in the sense in which the Special Theory of Relativity is 'complete' and the General Theory is deeply developed. This, you understand, is my personal evaluation."

Another pause, and then the bombshell:

"I have thought this over," he said, "and have come up with a few fairly well-defined memory impressions of ideas and calculations on a project which quite possibly developed into a full-scale ship experiment."

He was hedging, I thought. I could tell because his words had begun to take on that guarded, carefully chosen quality.

"I have impressions of wartime conferences

in which I recall the participation of naval officers. In relation to the project in which you are interested, my memory persistently suggests an inception distinctly earlier than 1943, perhaps as early as 1939 or 1940 when Einstein was concerned with ideas in physical theory brought to him by physicists and others who had military applications in mind. . . .

"By recalling a number of [events], I think I can say with some degree of certainty that the proposal initiators were Einstein and [Rudolph] Ladenburg. I do not know who should be named first; and if the initiators were 'Blank,' Einstein, and Ladenburg, then I cannot now recall Blank's identity. I do know that Professor Ladenburg . . . had known Einstein since Switzerland in 1908. He was a reticent, meticulous sort of character with old Prussian aristocratic manners; but he was deeply respected by colleagues as a relaxed 'lone thinker' and worker."

During the course of this revelation, Rinehart had gotten to his feet and was now peering nervously out the window through a small chink in the venetian blinds. Apparently satisfied that our solitude wasn't about to be disturbed, he went on with his story.

"Getting back to Ladenburg, he was quite an expert in the area of mines, torpedoes, and countermeasures against them. I particularly remember a large conference or colloquium, during which a possible German weapon development came into discussion. My superior, the physicist, Dr. W. W. Albrecht [pseudonym], was impatient with some not very bright ideas put forward by some uninhibited 'names and ranks.' Albrecht broke into the discussion by calling on Ladenburg as 'the only person present who has had German military experience,' and referred to him as having been a submarine commander or something during the Great War. I suspect that this remark may have been intended more for its possible shock effect than as a statement of fact. I'm not entirely certain whether Ladenburg ever was a submarine officer of any sort or not; but it really doesn't matter since the tactic itself proved successful. Ladenburg stood up stiffly at this point and proceeded to lay out in a few assured-sounding sentences what the Germans had and could do. The 'names and ranks' promptly subsided, and the conference went back on track. Someone remarked to me later something to the effect that you would think that Ladenburg had just walked out of the Germans' front office."

Rinehart chuckled lightly to himself and continued.

"Ladenburg had been working in the Princeton physics laboratory on fission experiments in the summer and fall of 1939. I think I read somewhere that he is thought to have discussed these with Einstein. In any event, I think I recall from about 1940 that the proposal I associate with the pre-ship projects was supposed to be the result of discussions between Ladenburg and Einstein on using electromagnetic fields to counter mines and torpedoes, and

Dr. John von Neumann.

that . . . Einstein himself [was] the actual proposal writer. . . .

"Einstein and Ladenburg were forward people in advancing project proposals, but they were quite content to be rear-rankers in dealing with the brass. Von Neumann [Dr. John von Neumann, 1903–57, early pioneer of the digital computer and well-known mathematician] was a modest-seeming person who found it interesting to try to influence and activate the powerful. On some proposal, very possibly the one at hand, von Neumann was asked by the Navy brass whether he was talking about this war or the next. . . .

"Anyway, it was von Neumann who talked to Dr. Albrecht on this proposal, and it was one or the other of them who obtained an indication of future cooperation on it from the Naval Research Laboratory. The proposal partly overlapped ideas developed by the physicist R. H. Kent [Robert Harrington Kent, 1886–1961, noted American theoretical and research physicist] many years before during the course of design and experimental work with the solenoid chronograph. If you think about the principle of the solenoid chronograph, you will see why work with it would suggest all kinds of ideas about detection and defense against missiles by the use of electromagnetic fields."

Rinehart evidently assumed that I knew what a solenoid chronograph was. I didn't, but an interruption at this point didn't seem in order. He continued:

"I think it was Kent who was the inventor of the solenoid chronograph. He was at least its most important development man, and the first to use it to measure accurate drag coefficients for projectiles at high Mach number. He was likely to demonstrate the principle by dropping a magnetized iron slug through a solenoid and showing the current waveform resulting on an oscilloscope. If the audience included physicists, he also dropped the solenoid past the slug and obtained the same results. He then said, 'See, the laws of physics are the same for any pair of inertial coordinate systems.' This, of course, was Einstein's second postulate in his 1905 paper on Special Relativity.

"I recall a story circulating to the effect that after learning of von Neumann's interest in such a project, Kent tried to locate some idea papers he had written on some similar topic away back when. According to the story, which I got from a friend of mine who was working in Kent's department down in Maryland at the time, his files had been moved from one location to another on several occasions, and what he wanted was not to be immediately located. Kent's reaction to this annoyance was said to have been to impress his entire office staff to aid in the search—a process which resulted in the entire place being literally turned upside down and creating one devil of a mess. Anyhow, a pair of ancient brown papers was unearthed at long last from a file and presented to him triumphantly.

"Following this incident, Kent proceeded to talk to physicists and engineers he had known many years before, possibly as far back as his Harvard days, but more likely from association during the First World War, or shortly after. One of these, I believe, was Professor Charles M. Allen."

"Allen?" I started. "Any connection to the *Carl* M. Allen we discussed in our correspondence?"

Rinehart stared at me and laughed. "No," he said, "I don't think so. Not *Carl* Allen ... *Charles* Allen. Charles Metcalf Allen, I think. This fellow was a professor in hydraulic engineering up at Worcester Polytechnic at the time. Knew a great deal about ships, models, mines, and so on, and would have been a likely candidate with whom to discuss ideas. I must admit that I hadn't considered the similarity of names before; but no, I don't think they're connected. At least not closely, anyway. Professor Allen was an old man then, and quite distinguished. He must have been at least seventy when the war began.

"Now that I think about it, I feel confident that the idea of producing the necessary electromagnetic field for experimental purposes by means of the principles of resonance was also initially suggested by Kent—possibly as a result of these discussions with Professor Allen. I recall some computations about this in relation to a model experiment [i.e., an experiment conducted using scale models rather than real ships] which was in view at the time. I have the impression that the Navy 'took hold' not long after these discussions between Kent and Allen. It also seems likely to me that 'foiling radar' was discussed at some later point in relation to this project. I recall this vaguely in relation to some conference.

"To get back on the right track, however. It was most probably von Neumann who proposed the idea for such a project to what was then, in late '39 or early '40, known as the National Defense Research Committee (NDRC), and it seems likely that Professor Kent gave him considerable support in pushing the proposal along. My own personal contact with it did not come until after these initial steps had been taken and the NDRC people had expressed an interest in pursuing it further."

"I wonder," I broke in, "what do you suppose was the reason for their interest in such a project?"

"Well," he replied, "that's simple enough to answer. From its beginnings this was strictly a defensive-measures type project rather than any attempt at creating offensive capabilities. The initial idea seems to have been aimed at using strong electromagnetic fields to deflect incoming projectiles, especially torpedoes, away from a ship by means of creating an intense electromagnetic field around that ship. This was later extended to include a study of the idea of producing optical invisibility by means of a similar field in the air rather than in the water.

"One day, probably early in 1940, at about 8:00 in the morning, Dr. Albrecht, my superior, arrived in his office to find two or possibly three visitors from NDRC already waiting for him. Since this was not an especially unusual occurrence, I didn't think too much about it until about 9:30 or so, when Captain Gibbons came down the hall and put his head in at the door. He put up his finger, which was the signal for me to come out into the hall as he had something to say which could not be said in front of the whole office. I remember this because I was involved with some rather complicated theoretical work at the time and was busy talking to a computer on the telephone." (Ed. note: These were the days before the advent of electronic computers. The "computer" referred to here was a person who was particularly adept at performing rapid computations mentally.)

"Realizing that the matter must be of some importance, I broke off my work and went out into the hallway. Gibbons led me down the hall to the boss's office, where I found myself in the midst of a conference already in progress between these two (or was it three?) NDRC people on the one hand, and Dr. Albrecht and Dr. von Neumann on the other. Von Neumann didn't stay long, however, and his purpose there may have been only to introduce the NDRC people to Albrecht and to briefly outline what the meeting was all about. He was frequently involved in carrying messages to and from Washington involving various NDRC and military projects, and so this would have been a normal role for him even if he hadn't been personally interested. Not to be overlooked, however, are the obvious advantages of such a position for promoting those ideas in which he *was* interested—this project included. In any event, he left the room soon after I arrived."

Rinehart was up again and headed for another look out the window. Apparently satisfied at what he saw (or didn't see), he resumed his story.

"There was quite a discussion in progress when I came in concerning what was eventually to become this project you are interested in. Albrecht was the type who felt an obligation to stay in a discussion to keep it going, and frequently when he wanted some computations done he would send out for someone rather than leave the discussion to do them himself. Apparently he felt that I was the only one of sufficient background in gravity and relativity to get mathematical results of the type he wanted in a hurry without asking too many questions about it, so I was called in.

"Albrecht had two or three sheets of paper, one of which had on it the small, spirally handwriting peculiar to only Dr. Einstein. He wanted these sheets looked into while he was busy talking to these people, and he continued to try to talk to them while at the same time giving me instructions as to what I was supposed to do. He had on one part of a sheet a radiation-wave equation, and on the left side were a series of half-finished scratches. With these he pushed over a rather detailed report on naval degaussing equipment and poked fingers at it here and there while I marked with pencil where he pointed. Then Albrecht said could I see what would be needed to get a bending of light by, oh, I think 10 percent, and would I try to complete this enough to make a small table or two concerning it. I said, 'How long have I got?' And he said, 'Not long.' Then he looked at the others and they started to talk and spoiled his train of thought.

"I think," he continued, "that the conversation at this point had turned to the principles of resonance and how the intense fields which would be required for such an experiment might be achieved using this principle. I didn't really get an answer as to how long I had, but Albrecht nodded his head at me to go out and get to work; so I went back down the hall to Captain Gibbons and said to him, 'When do you think W. W. [Albrecht] has got to have this?' Gibbons thought a moment and said, 'I'll take them to the Officers' Club and you can have through the lunch hour, but nothing more.' By one or two o'clock, no more.

"Albrecht's notes were not easy to follow, and I think that anyone with less of a mathematical and theoretical background than I had would have been pretty well lost. As it was, I saw what it was he was trying to do. This is not to say that there weren't other men in the department who could have handled it just as well given the proper time, but Albrecht wanted to have figures on it right away and so it was left to me.

"It must have been a quick lunch, because Gibbons was back at 1:15 and I was still after it. I said to him that I wanted to make a memo out of it and a typed copy, and that I could have it ready by 3:00 if he could delay them that long. Gibbons said that wouldn't do, and that there was to be absolutely *no* typed copy. It was to be in pencil as it stood. 'Miracles,' I said, 'Always they want miracles!...Listen,' I said, 'Give me twenty or twenty-five minutes more and I'll see what I can do.' Gibbons wasn't happy about it, but there wasn't much else to be done if he wanted results. I got the twenty minutes.

"Somehow, I managed to finish a couple of small tables and a few sentences of explanation and brought all back as a memo. We went in to Albrecht, who looked it all over and said, 'You did all this regarding intensities [of the field] at differing distances from the [ship's] beam, but you don't seem to pick up anything fore and aft.' Albrecht always was a stickler for detail. I hadn't included this because I wasn't quite sure what it was he wanted exactly, and because there was more work involved than there had been time to do it in. All I had was the points of greatest curvatures right off the ship's beam opposite this equipment. My problem was in trying to orient what Albrecht wanted. Einstein's notes were a good deal clearer than Albrecht's, but I wouldn't have dared to tell him so.

"Now that I think of it," he reflected, "it is possible that von Neumann was in the office by accident that day, and that Oswald Veblen [one of von Neumann's associates] had brought it down. It is also possible that the NDRC men brought it down themselves. What Albrecht wanted to do was to find out enough to verify the strength of the field and the practical probability of bending light sufficiently to get the desired 'mirage' effect. God knows they had no idea what the final results would be. If they had, it would have ended there. But, of course, they didn't.

"I think the prime movers at this point were the NDRC and someone like Ladenburg or von Neumann who came up with ideas and had no hesitancy in talking about them before doing any computations at all. They talked with Einstein about this and Einstein considered it and took it far enough to figure out the order of magnitude he would need on intensity, and then spoke to von Neumann about what would be the best outfit to look into it as a practical possibility. That's how we got involved in it. I am not exactly certain when the Naval Research Lab came into it, but I do know that Commander Parsons, one of the top Navy scientists, talked quite often to Albrecht, and it is possible that something concerning the use of a ship came up in that way.

"The only thing I did with this on paper was to put together Albrecht's few scratch equations and make several small tables. Afterwards I can remember a couple of times when expansions on these equations of mine came up in meetings, and so I was able to maintain a certain level of awareness as to what was being done in other circles even though I wasn't involved directly."

I said, "Do you recall what the code name of this project might have been?"

Rinehart thought a moment in silence. When the answer came, I got the impression again that he was choosing his words with care.

"You must remember," he said, "that Albrecht and Gibbons treated this on a strictly no-copy basis—that is to say, memos in pencil only with no typewritten or carbon copies. I seem to recall once using the term 'deflection' in a heading; I can remember that. I can also remember a point a little later when I suggested in a meeting of some sort that an easier way to make a ship vanish was a light air blanket, and I wondered why such a fairly complicated theoretical affair was under consideration. Albrecht took off his glasses at that point and commented that the trouble with having me at a conference was that I was good at getting them off the topic. A code name would have had to have been selected by NDRC, and in all probability there was no code name at this point. I don't recall whether I encountered a code name for this project at a later date or not, although somewhere in the back of my mind I seem to want to associate the terms 'Rainbow' or 'Mirage' with it. Memory is vague and I may be quite a bit off the track

MOST SECRET

Copy No.

Attention is drawn to the Penalties attaching to any infraction of the Official Secrets Acts

INTER-SERVICES CODE-WORD INDEX

This Index will be kept in a safe when not in use

Issued under the authority of the Inter-Services Security Board, War Office.

1st *September*, 1941

C.C.S. 368/15.

Ciphering Numeral.	Code Word.	Block Number.	Ciphering Numeral.	Code Word.	Block Number.
7400	PUSSYFOOT	374	7450	RACQUET	266
7401	PUTNEY	590	7451	RADCLIFFE	748
7402	PUTRID	287	7452	RADFORD	854
7403	PUTTENHAM	804	7453	RADIAL	266
7404	PUZZLE	181	7454	RADIATION	324
7405	PYGMALION	164	7455	RADIATOR	491
7406	PYRAMID	170	7456	RADIO	2
7407	PYRITES	979	7457	RADISHES	304
7408	PYRRHUS	170	7458	RADIUM	430
7409	PYTHAGORAS	594	7459	RADNAGE	722

The Inter Services Code-Word Index containing the code word "Rainbow," which may have been the project name for the Philadelphia Experiment. When first contacted, the National Archives reported no record of Project Rainbow and no knowledge of an index of projects, but when the name "Rainbow" was later given to the National Archives this proof print of the index was obtained.

7410	PYTHON	288	**7460**	RADNOR	883
7411	QUADRANGLE	149	7461	RAEBURN	748
7412	QUADRUPED	548	7462	RAFFIA	266
7413	QUAGGA	619	7463	RAFFLE	422
7414	QUAGMIRE	126	7464	RAFTER	287
7415	QUAINTON	871	7465	RAGAMUFFIN	126
7416	QUARRY	143	7466	RAGMAN	181
7417	QUARTER	454	7467	RAGOUT	432
7418	QUARTERMAIN	388	7468	RAILWAY	33
7419	QUEEN	17	7469	RAIMENT	933
7420	QUEENBEE	643	**7470**	RAINBOW	334
7421	QUENCH	234	7471	RAINHAM	827
7422	QUICK	665	7472	RAISIN	229
7423	QUICKFIRE	104	7473	RAKEOFF	988
7424	QUICKLIME	548	7474	RAKISH	544
7425	QUICKSAND	561	7475	RALLY	188
7426	QUINCES	304	7476	RALPH	44
7427	QUINN	365	7477	RALSTON	827
7428	QUINTAL	123	7478	RAMBLER	431
7429	QUINTIN	266	7479	RAMESES	600
7430	QUIRK	585	**7480**	RAMIFICATION	63
7431	QUISLING	119	7481	RAMMER	288
7432	QUITMAN	659	7482	RAMONA	457
7433	QUIVER	129	7483	RAMOSE	158
7434	QUIXOTE	29	7484	RAMPAGE	**434**
7435	QUIZZY	173	7485	RAMPART	556
7436	QUOIT	393	7486	RAMPION	22
7437	QUORUM	563	7487	RAMPIRE	233
7438	QUOTATION	563	7488	RAMROD	143
7439	RABBITS	323	7489	RAMSDEN	853
7440	RABBLE	123	**7490**	RAMSHACKLE	561
7441	RABELAIS	450	7491	RAMSHORN	854
7442	RABID	652	7492	RAMSON	267
7443	RACEFIELD	559	7493	RANCHER	534
7444	RACHEL	447	7494	RANCID	141
7445	RACING	308	7495	RANDALSTOWN	738
7446	RACKETEER	487	7496	RANDOM	451
7447	RACKHAM	883	7497	RANELAGH	590
7448	RACONTEUR	266	7498	RANGE	19
7449	RACOON	266	7499	RANJI	601

with these. I just don't remember.

"I do remember being at at least one other conference where this matter was a topic on the agenda. During this one we were trying to bring out some of the more obvious—to us—side effects that would be created by such an experiment. Among these would be a 'boiling' of the water, ionization of the surrounding air, and even a 'Zeemanizing' of the atoms; all of which would tend to create extremely unsettled conditions. No one at this point had ever considered the possibility of interdimensional effects or mass displacement. Scientists generally thought of such things as belonging more to science fiction than to science in the 1940s. In any event, at some point during all this, I received a strong putdown from Albrecht, who broke in with something to the effect that 'Why don't you just leave these experimental people alone so they can go ahead with their project. That's what we have them for!'

"One of the problems involved was that the ionization created by the field tended to cause an uneven refraction of the light. The original concepts that were brought down to us before the conference were laid out very nicely and neatly, but both Albrecht and Gleason and I warned that according to our calculations the result would not be a steady mirage effect, but rather a 'moving back and forth' displacement caused by certain inherent tendencies of the AC field which would tend to create a confused area rather than a complete absence of color. 'Confused' may well have been an understatement, but it seemed appropriate at the time. Immediately out beyond this confused area ought to be a shimmering, and far outside ought to be a static field. At any rate, our warning on this, which ultimately went to NDRC, was that all this ought to be taken into account and the whole thing looked at with some care. We also felt that with proper effort some of these problems could be overcome ... and that a resonant frequency could probably be found that would possibly control the visual apparent internal oscillation so that the shimmering would be at a much slower rate.... I don't know how far those who were working on this aspect of the problem ever got with it.

"I also remember a couple of meetings later which dealt with this topic, but memory is hazy on details. Another thing I recall strongly is that for a few weeks after the meeting in Albrecht's office we kept getting requests for tables having to do with resonant frequencies of light in optical ranges. These were frequently without explanation attached, but it seems likely that there was some connection here."

Rinehart began to look around the room nervously as if perhaps he had said too much, but he plunged on.

"I keep wanting to place C. M. Allen in a position of having to do with the model experiments. These may have been carried out at the Taylor Model Basin; but then again maybe not, since I'm not sure whether the capabilities to do so existed at this facility yet or not. Some work was most likely conducted at the Anacostia Bay site—which was the same site used for much of the early radar work."

"How do you suppose they went about getting a ship to actually try this out on?" I asked. "Someone somewhere certainly must have stuck his neck out for this thing."

"That's a good question. I have twice considered suggesting to you that Captain Parsons [William S. Parsons, the same man who personally armed the atomic bomb aboard the aircraft *Enola Gay* before the drop on Hiroshima in 1945] may have played a role in seeing that this project was a 'ship experiment' and not merely a model experiment.... I remember from a conference on a different project in 1939 that my superiors felt that no one but Parsons could possibly prevail upon the Bureau of Ships to permit a trial of a new instrument on board ship. At that time Captain Parsons was Commander Parsons...the most notable of Naval Academy graduates with actual standing as a research scientist. He walked into conferences followed by two or three lieutenants whom I remember only faintly....

"With regard to the merchant ship which you indicated may have been used as an observer ship...I feel that Admiral Jerry Land, head of the U.S. Martime Commission, may have been helpful here. He was what you might call the 'hard-boiled' type, but was frequently willing to be helpful—especially when the Navy wasn't.

There were, for example, numerous instances when we were more successful in prevailing upon the USMC to allow us to place experimental equipment on board merchant ships for trials than we were in persuading the Navy to allow us to use their ships.

"In this particular type of experimental project, I feel certain that Admiral Land was asked and urged to get a ship and crew with which nothing could go wrong. According to a friend of mine, an attempt was made to get a good choice on this so as not to embarrass Admiral Land in front of the Navy. Very possibly, according to my friend, the crew placed aboard this ship consisted of hand-picked sailors, at least some of whom would have been verterans of the Murmansk run and so would have been of the most courageous sort."

And so, in essence, ends the bulk of Dr. Rinehart's fascinating story—all except for one further bit of information which has purposely been laid aside until a later chapter. Following the interview which produced most of the foregoing material, Moore continued to maintain contact with him on a more or less regular basis right up to the time of his unexpected death a little more than five months later. Generally these contacts were friendly rather than professional, but occasionally some forgotten bit of information was produced which proved useful or interesting. One such even seems worth repeating here as a sort of postscript.

The story concerns one of the numerous American scientists of German origin who had worked in Germany before the coming of Hitler, and who had fled here to escape possible persecution. It seems that the War Department was particularly fond of several of these scientists and endeavored to consult with them on a more or less regular basis to seek out their opinions about the various scientific developments that the Germans were thought to be working on.

In one of the last letters Moore received from him, Dr. Rinehart recalled being at a certain conference where one of the topics under discussion was this particular project. At some point during the discussion, the German scientist in question was asked by one of the Navy officers present whether he thought that the Germans might not be working on anything of a similar nature.

According to Dr. Rinehart, the German hesitated only a moment before replying in his heavily inflected but otherwise perfect English that "the officer should realize that while American naval scientific personnel might well be appropriately characterized as 'stick-in-the-muds' as far as certain matters might be concerned, it was infinitely better than the German navy in others—the case in point as an example. Had someone dared to suggest such a project to the German Naval command," the German scientist went on, "he would have been politely but firmly reminded that his time might better be spent thinking about weapons of offense rather than measures for defense against an inferior enemy."

All of this tends to reinforce the possibility that there was indeed a project in the works which could easily have, and very possibly did, develop into something of the magnitude of the Philadelphia Experiment.

But an important and pertinent question remains unanswered: How did Carlos Allende manage to learn sufficient details about these obviously quite complex and highly secret goings-on to enable him to write his series of letters to Dr. Jessup?

Unfortunately the picture puzzle is not quite complete enough to enable us to arrive at a concrete answer regarding this particular point. However, this does not preclude an attempt to make the best guess possible based on the information obtained from Dr. Rinehart on the topic.

As we have shown, there can be no doubt that the man who calls himself Carlos Allende did indeed serve as a seaman aboard the *S.S. Andrew Furuseth*. Knowing what we do now, it seems almost certain that he did indeed witness at least some of the things he wrote about in his letters. That these events disturbed him greatly is self-evident.

With this in mind, we can safely conjecture that finding some logical explanation for what he had seen remained foremost in his mind. At least he appears to have made a point of dis-

cussing the topic with every person of scientific
background that he happened to meet; and since
he was wont to seek out these people whenever
possible by attending public lectures on scientific topics, he most likely picked up quite a
store of knowledge in the process—a sort of self-
education in things scientific.

The bonanza he was looking for came when
a chance meeting led to what became a short
but highly productive acquaintance with Dr.
Rinehart, the one man who could fill him in on
some of the details of the ship experiment that
had long troubled his conscious thoughts. Dr.
Rinehart, while not willing to impart too many
details of the affair lest official secrecy be com-
promised, nonetheless let enough of the cat out
of the bag to cause Carlos to worry that ideas
which could lead to more of such research might
still be lurking in the back of certain military-
scientific minds. When Jessup's *The Case for
the UFO* was published not too long thereafter,
Allende began to fear that this book might possibly get the ball rolling again.

The fear turned to sheer horror when, following his discussions with Dr. Rinehart and
shortly after reading Jessup's book, he happened to attend one of Jessup's public lectures.
When during the course of his presentation,
Jessup admonished his audience to push for
more government funds and government research into the Unified Field Theory, Allende
was stunned. It was in such a state of mind that
Allende wrote his second letter to Dr. Jessup,

in which he laid out the facts concerning what he thought he had witnessed during the war and then described the possible consequences of such research in graphic detail. Allende had no way of knowing that his "friend, Dr. Franklin Reno" regularly used a pseudonym which had originally been inspired by a road sign. Nor had he any idea that through his reference to this individual in a letter which he had every reason to assume would remain confidential he was perpetuating the use of an alias which would continue to plague and puzzle researchers for many years to come.

One thing is certain: Considering the degree of publicity and notoriety that the Allende letters have attained over the years, had Allende ever been able to identify Dr. Rinehart by his real name, it is almost certain that the reputation of this scientist would have long since been demolished by the rest of the scientific establishment. He may have also considered the possibility of threats to his privacy or his life.

Dr. Rinehart, however, is not the only person known to have played a part in the planning of the Philadelphia Experiment. Further research has turned up at least one other who not only had a part in the project, but may ultimately have discovered a most intriguing method of putting his knowledge of force fields to practical use.

CHAPTER 10

The Force Fields of Townsend Brown

Might there be any practical applications for energies and force fields of the type reportedly utilized to create invisibility during the Philadelphia Experiment? Could these applications include possible methods of propulsion, of the same type that Morris Jessup suspected was being utilized by whoever or whatever was piloting the UFOs? We can gain insight into these questions by examining the life and career of an obscure but extremely brilliant American physicist and inventor named Thomas Townsend Brown—a man who, like Dr. Rinehart, was ultimately destined to play a part in the project which led to the actual experiment itself.

Born into a prominent Zanesville, Ohio, family in 1905, Townsend Brown displayed an early interest in space travel—a topic considered sheerest fantasy in the days when there were those who looked askance at the Wright brothers' successes. Nonetheless, young Brown retained his interest and enjoyed occupying himself with electronics. It was his youthful toying with the infant ideas of radio and electromagnetism that provided a background which was to prove invaluable to him in later years; and it was during the course of this "experimenting" that Brown somehow acquired a Coolidge X-ray tube—an item that was to lead him to make a most startling discovery.

X-rays (or Roentgen rays) were indeed mysterious forces in those days (in fact, the American physical chemist William D. Coolidge had only just invented the Coolidge tube itself in 1913), and even legitimate science was just beginning to learn anything about them. Brown wasn't interested in X-rays for themselves but he did think that a key to space flight might be found there. And toward that end he set up an experiment to determine whether there might be a useful force of some sort exerted by the rays emanating from his Coolidge tube.

Doing something that no scientist of his day had thought of, Brown mounted his Coolidge tube in extremely delicate balance and began "testing" for results. He was unable to detect any measurable force exerted by the X-rays regardless of which way he turned his apparatus, but suddenly he became aware of a very strange quality of the tube itself: Every time it was turned on, the tube seemed to exhibit a motion of its own—a "thrust" of some sort, just as if the apparatus were trying to move! Investigating further, Brown had to spend considerable time and effort before the explanation finally became apparent. This newfound phenomenon had nothing whatsoever to do with the X-rays—it was the high voltage being used to produce the rays which was behind it!

Brown now undertook a whole new series of experiments designed to determine the exact nature of this new "force" he had discovered, and after much effort he finally succeeded in developing a device which he optimistically chose to call a "gravitor." His invention looked like nothing more than a Bakelite case some 12 inches long and 4 inches square; but when placed on a scale and connected with a 100-kilovolt power source the apparatus proceeded to either gain or lose about 1 percent of its weight, depending on the polarity used.

Brown was sure he had discovered a new electrical principle, but he did not know just what to do with it. And in spite of the fact that there were a few newspaper accounts of his work, no scientist of any stature expressed any interest in his discovery—not entirely surprising when one considers that Townsend Brown was only then on the verge of graduating from high school.

In 1922, Brown entered the California Institute of Technology (Caltech) at Pasadena. He spent his first year courting the favor of his

Townsend Brown. (*NICAP*)

professors, among whom was the late physicist and Nobel laureate Dr. Robert A. Millikan. However, his success in convincing his instructors of his excellence as a lab man was more than offset by his complete failure to gain even the slightest measure of recognition for his ideas about electrogravity. His teachers, steeped in the rigors of nineteenth-century scientific discipline, steadfastly refused to admit that such a thing could even exist; they were not interested in new or revolutionary concepts.

Undaunted, Brown transferred to Kenyon College, Gambier, Ohio, in 1923, remaining there only one year and then transferring to Denison University at Granville, Ohio, where he studied as an electronics resident in the Department of Physics under Dr. Paul Alfred Biefeld, professor of physics and astronomy and former classmate, in Switzerland, of Dr. Einstein (one of only eight).

Unlike Dr. Millikan at Caltech, Dr. Biefeld proved to be interested in Brown's discovery, and together the two of them—professor and student—experimented with charged electrical capacitors and developed a principle of physics which came to be tentatively known as the Biefeld-Brown Effect. Basically, the "effect" concerned the observed tendency of a highly charged electrical condenser to exhibit motion toward its positive pole—the same motion observed earlier by Brown with his Coolidge tube.

Following the completion of his formal education, Townsend Brown joined the staff of the Swazey Observatory in Ohio, where he remained for some four years and during which time he married. In 1930, Brown left the staff of Swazey to sign on with the Naval Research Laboratory in Washington, D.C. as a specialist in radiation, field physics, and spectroscopy.

It was during this phase of his life that he participated as staff physicist in the U.S. Navy Department's International Gravity Expedition to the West Indies in 1932, and as physicist in the Johnson-Smithsonian Deep Sea Expedition of 1933. Later that same year the continuing depression caused the inevitable budget cutbacks, and Brown had to abandon what had looked like a promising career at the Naval Research Lab (NRL) in search of greener pastures. Much like Drs. Jessup and Rinehart, Brown turned to the government for work. He joined the Navy Reserve and, finding scientific jobs of any type to be scarce, landed a position first as a soil engineer for the Federal Emergency Relief Administration and later as an administrator for the Civilian Conservation Corps in Ohio.

Daytime jobs during the 1930s, however, did not prevent him from continuing his study of physics in general and the Biefeld-Brown Effect in particular during available evening and weekend hours. With the passage of time, the original "gravitor" design saw numerous improvements.

In 1939, Brown, now a lieutenant in the Navy Reserve, moved to Maryland to become a material engineer for the Glenn L. Martin Company of Baltimore (later Martin Aerospace). He was there only a matter of months, however, when he was called upon by the Navy to become officer in charge of magnetic and acoustic minesweeping research and development under the Bureau of Ships.

It was shortly after receiving this appointment that Brown came into contact with the early development stages of the project that may have become the Philadelphia Experiment. According to Dr. Rinehart:

"I believe that when he [Brown] was brought back from Martin into the Bureau of Ships as officer in charge of acoustic and magnetic minesweeping, all projects that Ross Gunn, then director of the Naval Research Laboratory, thought interesting were brought up to him because of his background in physics. This is where he got involved in your 'project'—this is his beginning point.

"His section would have covered every new thing that would have come in regarding this, and they tried to get a good man to work on it. This was Brown. He was brought in because they were short of people—especially good ones—and needed someone who would not be a stick-in-the-mud with regard to the things they were thinking about. He undoubtedly would also have conferred with Captain Parsons on this project.

"Although my personal relationship with Brown never came any closer than an occasional few words (he was in a totally different department, you will recall), I can clearly remember his presence at the same table with me during several conferences at which this project was discussed. I don't believe I ever spoke to him more than once or twice at any length. He was a rather shy and retiring individual, as I recall; a man whose ideas and efforts were frequently more defended by his friends and associates than by himself."

It is questionable whether Brown was really ever very heavily involved in the Philadelphia Experiment project. Although he tends to be rather unspecific on the point, it seems virtually certain that he would have had to have been involved in at least some capacity, since a great portion of the work of his research team was carried out in the related area of ship degaussing. He also performed what he characterizes as "some very valuable high-vacuum work."

In any event, his service with the Bureau of Ships, where he presided over the expenditure of some $50 million for research and at least a dozen junior Ph.D.s, can be regarded as exemplary to say the least. It was not to be exceptionally long-lived, however, for in the general shake-up that followed Pearl Harbor, he was transferred, with the rank of lieutenant commander, to Norfolk to continue his research while heading up the Navy's Atlantic Fleet Radar School there.

According to another source of information, it was while serving in this assignment that he put forth some suggestions on how electromagnetic fields might be utilized to achieve partial radar invisibility, especially in air-to-sea situations. However, whether these ideas might possibly have been incorporated directly into the ongoing research into the Philadelphia Experiment project or whether they were ever even acted upon at all is not known. Brown was not the type to push his own ideas too hard unless they seemed to meet with the willing approval of others.

In spite of his reticence, however, he was a willing and dedicated worker who continued to serve his country well during the next two years. Unfortunately, by December 1943, his long and hard work and his personal disappointment at the failure of his projects to gain proper recognition had finally taxed him to the limit. He suffered a nervous collapse that sent him home to rest. Upon the recommendation of a team of naval physicians, retirement from the service quickly followed.

An interesting sidelight at this point is that

Riley Crabb has steadfastly claimed that the cause of Brown's breakdown was directly related to the Philadelphia Experiment. Certainly severe repercussions would have almost certainly followed any disastrous physical or psychological results of the sort reported to have been suffered by the crew of the DE 173, and the head of any person responsible for conducting such a project would undoubtedly have been placed on the block as a result. If such a thing did occur, it is not too difficult to imagine the extreme mental pressures that would result. However, in all fairness to Brown, it should be noted that we have been totally unable to discover anything at all which would even begin to substantiate such a conjecture.

In any event, after six months of rest, the late spring of 1944 found Brown working as a radar consultant for the advanced-design section of Lockheed-Vega Aircraft Corporation in California. Colleagues there found him to be much the same as described by Dr. Rinehart, referring to him as "a quiet, modest, retiring man...a brilliant solver of engineering problems" and "exactly the sort one expects to find in important research installations." More important, he was still working on his gravitor device, although (interestingly) he chose not to speak in terms of gravity when describing it. Instead, he seemed to prefer the more scientific but decidedly less sensational term "stress in dielectrics."

After leaving Lockheed, Brown went to Hawaii to live and to continue his research. It was during this time, partly thanks to the efforts of an old friend, A. L. Kitselman, who was then teaching calculus at Pearl Harbor, that Brown's gravitor apparatus, somewhat improved over earlier versions, came to the interest of Admiral Arthur W. Radford, Commander in Chief of the U.S. Pacific Fleet (and later to become Chairman of the Joint Chiefs of Staff under President Eisenhower, 1953–57). As a result of Admiral Radford's interest, Brown was temporarily accorded consultant status to the Pearl Harbor Navy Yard; but in spite of the fact that the former lieutenant commander was well treated by his Navy friends, it appears from the evidence that they considered his invention rather more of an interesting curiosity than any sort of key to space or interdimensional travel. Perhaps had Brown been more of a salesman than a scientist, things might have been different; although it is also possible that the Navy had seen more than its share of force-field research during the war and was keeping its distance from any more such projects for obvious reasons. (Carlos Allende's statement that "the Navy fears to use such results" returns to mind at this point.)

In the meantime, increased UFO activity at the turn of the decade had captured Brown's personal interest. Eagerly following the controversy as it raged among the military and scientific community in the late '40s and early '50s, Brown postulated that perhaps with the proper worldwide scientific approach the dilemma surrounding the power source of the UFO might be solved. In those days his belief in the abilities of modern science was such that he even dared to speculate on the possibility of a quick solution, provided that the proper resources and manpower were poured into it. Of course, he remained constantly aware of the possibility that through his own efforts at research into electro-gravitics he had hit upon one of the keys to the mystery.

Moving to Cleveland in 1952, Brown conceived of a project he called Winterhaven, an idea which he hoped (with proper refinements) could be offered for sale to the military establishment. Through patient research, he succeeded in improving the lift force of his gravitor apparatus until it was such that it could lift significantly more than its own weight—a success that should have raised the eyebrows of any respectable scientist or Pentagon official, but apparently didn't, even though the apparatus involved was quite sophisticated and, as we shall see, the demonstrations most impressive.

Theoretically speaking, Brown attempted to explain his results in terms of Unified Field physics. The point of departure between Brown and most of orthodox science is that Brown firmly believes in the existence of an observable coupling effect between gravity and electricity and that this coupling effect is precisely what is being demonstrated by his devices. In other words, he contends that the Biefeld-Brown Effect not only represents a proved and demonstrable link between electricity and gravitation, but represents one which can actually be harnessed and utilized for propulsion purposes both within and outside of the earth's atmosphere. The similarities of all of this to the concepts reportedly utilized in the Philadelphia Experiment project is readily apparent.

A "dielectric" is defined as a material which has the unique ability of absorbing electrical energy or "charge" without ordinarily passing this energy on to neighboring materials. Some dielectrics are able to absorb enormous quantities of electrical energy (also referred to as "elastic stress") without discharging, provided that the energy is fed into the dielectric slowly and at low potential. Still others can be charged and discharged at extremely high potential at a rate of several thousand times each second. Townsend Brown concerned himself principally with this latter type. Using just such a dielectric, Brown constructed disc-shaped (or saucer-shaped) condensers, and, by applying various amounts of high-voltage direct current, witnessed the Biefeld-Brown Effect in action. With the proper construction and electrical potential (in the kilovolt range) the disc-shaped "airfoils" were made to fly under their own power, emitting a slight hum and a bluish electrical glow as they did so. More scientifically, perhaps, this process of "flight" might best be described as "motion under the influence of interaction between electrical and gravitational fields in the direction of the positive electrode."

In 1953, Brown succeeded in demonstrating in a laboratory setting the flight of disc-shaped airfoils 2 feet in diameter around a 20-foot-diameter circular course. The process involved tethering these saucer-shaped craft to a central pole by means of a wire through which the necessary direct-current potential was supplied at a rate of 50,000 volts with continuous input of 50 watts. The test produced an observable top speed of an amazing 17 feet per second (about 12 miles per hour).

Working with almost superhuman determination and at great cost to his personal finances, Brown soon succeeded in surpassing even this accomplishment. At his next display, he exhibited a set of discs 3 feet across flying a 50-foot-diameter course with results so spectacular that they were immediately classified. Even so, most of the scientists who witnessed the demonstrations remained skeptical and generally tended to attribute Brown's motive force to what they called an "electrical wind"—this in spite of the fact that it would have required a veritable "electrical hurricane" to produce the lift potential observed! Nonetheless, pitiful few gave any credence whatsoever to ideas that the Biefeld-Brown Effect might represent anything at all new to the world of physics. Government funding was sought to enable the work to continue, but in 1955, realizing that the money would not be forthcoming, a disgruntled Brown went to Europe in hopes that perhaps he might be able to generate a little more enthusiasm there.

Although demonstrations were given first in England, it was on the Continent, under the auspices of a French corporation, La Société Nationale de Construction Aéronautique Sud Ouest (SNCASO), that things really began to look promising. During a set of tests performed confidentially within the company's research laboratory, Brown succeeded in flying some of his discs in a high vacuum with amazing results. Brown was ecstatic, for not only had he succeeded in proving that his discs flew more efficiently *without* air, but he had also shown that the speed and efficiency of his "craft" could be increased by providing greater voltage to the dielectric plates. Contemporary accounts easily visualized speeds of several hundred miles per hour using voltages in the range of 100,000 to 200,000; and at least one writer spoke of a "flame jet generator" then in the planning stages which supposedly would be able to provide power potential up to 15 million volts! In fact, plans had been laid for the immediate construction of a large vacuum chamber and a 500,000-volt power supply when disaster struck the project in the form of a corporate merger. SNCASO had agreed to combine with a larger company, Sud Est. The president of the emerging company proceeded to demonstrate an appalling lack of interest in "these far-out propulsion research efforts" and favored instead an increased interest in "air frame manufacture." Consequently, all facilities ordered by the former president to carry forward the electrogravitic research work were summarily canceled and a thoroughly disappointed Brown was forced to return home to the U.S. in 1956.

Within a year's time Brown was busily engaged as chief research and development consultant for the Whitehall-Rand Project, a new antigravity investigation being conducted under the personal auspices of Agnew Bahnson, president of the Bahnson Company of Winston-Salem, North Carolina. Bahnson was something of a UFO buff who nurtured a personal desire to be the first man to set foot on the moon. Using his own funds, he constructed a well-equipped private laboratory and invited Brown to come down and consult. However, as fate would have it, just as things began to look good for the venture Mr. Bahnson, an experienced pilot, was killed under somewhat unusual circumstances when his private airplane reportedly struck a high-tension wire. Bahnson's heirs were not interested in the project and it was quickly stopped.

In 1958, believing he had finally generated enough momentum to go it alone, Townsend Brown organized his own corporation under the name Rand International Limited, and set himself up as president. Although numerous patents were applied for and granted both in the U.S. and abroad, and in spite of numerous patiently given demonstrations to interested governmental and corporate groups, success again eluded him. Curiously enough, such interest as he was able to generate seemed to melt away almost as fast as it developed—almost as if someone (or perhaps something?) was working against him. While the corporate framework of Rand International still exists, there has been little evident activity in recent years.

In the early '60s, Brown did a brief stint as physicist for Electrokinetics Inc. of Bala Cynwyd, Pa., and upon terminating his employment there, went into semi-retirement. Since then he has lived on in California, quietly pursuing his research in hopes that perhaps someday, with a little luck, the world will notice.

His most recent involvement is with a project "housed largely at Stanford Research Institute with additional assistance being provided by the University of California and the Ames Research Center of NASA." The object of the research, details of which are still largely under wraps, is to try to determine what connection, if any, there is between the earth's gravitational field and rock electricity (also known as petro-electricity). If Brown can achieve his hoped-for goal of proving that petroelectricity is "induced" by the earth's gravitational field, it would go a long way toward strengthening not only Unified Field concepts in general, but Brown's own personal theories on electrogravity as well.

This crystallizes the question indirectly posed by this entire chapter: Why indeed has Townsend Brown's promising life work gone virtually unnoticed for these past three decades? Even today Brown is still of the opinion that further research into the Biefeld-Brown Effect could lead to a sensational breakthrough in space propulsion methods—not to mention the more domestic variety—if appropriate funding could be made available. Granted, research is expensive. But is money the real reason for the apparent lack of interest? Or could it possibly be that the long shadow of a more-than-thirty-year-old ship experiment has succeeded in casting its pall over his efforts—perhaps even to the extent of "arranging" for the convenient demise of one of his most financially influential supporters? Or perhaps, as Brown himself suggests, the human race is not yet ready to accept such a revolutionary scientific concept.

However, as scientific research of the last few

years has strikingly indicated, some hitherto incredible concepts concerning space, matter, energy, and time have become generally accepted in the scientific community. One remembers Haldane's comment: "The universe is not only queerer than we imagine; it is queerer than we can imagine."

CHAPTER 11

The Reality
of the Impossible

Since the earliest days of human civilization, mankind has dreamed of finding ways to accomplish the seemingly impossible. Even the briefest examination of human records dating back thousands of years finds our ancestors preoccupied with dreams of being able to fly through the air like the birds, exploring the faraway surface of the moon, or traveling deep beneath the oceans of our planet. With the continuing technical advances of modern civilization, however, yesterday's dreams have rapidly become today's realities, and mankind has been forced to look elsewhere for the stuff dreams are made of.

Curiously enough, even with all of man's modern know-how, one of our most ancient dreams still remains unfulfilled and alive in our imaginations. Who among us has not dreamed at least once of becoming invisible and walking among his fellow men unseen and unsuspected? Usually thought of in ancient times as an ability reserved only for the gods, or to mortals such as Perseus provided with a special talisman, invisibility has more recently not only managed to find its way into the plots of countless books and magazine articles, but has even served as the central theme of a popular television series.

One especially attractive aspect is that of being able to create and maintain a state of invisibility in wartime. (Imagine the surprise of an enemy which has been lulled into believing that no one is there until the final moment of the attack!) It goes without saying that the advantages would be virtually unlimited—provided, of course, that it could be done. But suppose for a moment that the evidence which has been presented up to this point is correct and that somehow someone did discover that such a thing *is* possible—that, through proper utilization of electronics and force fields, invisibility *can* be created over a limited area for a limited period of time. Suppose that, as Dr. Rinehart indicated, such a discovery occurred either just before or during World War II, and suppose the proponents of it were successful in catching the ears of our nation's wartime military establishment. Where would be the most likely place to carry out a quick Top Secret testing program for such an obviously interesting system of electronic camouflage? On land? Possibly—but to what advantage? Even if a small section of land and buildings could be rendered invisible, any enemy knowing the coordinates of that location could bomb it anyway. Land tends to be immovable and generally an easy target—not to mention the fact that any successful land-based invisibility would not only be strictly defensive in its possibilities, but would have to be maintained on a round-the-clock basis (at least during the daylight hours) to be of any use. Land-based usage, therefore, does not seem to be the most desirable. Aircraft? Highly unlikely, considering the bulk and weight of electronics gear in the 1940s and the limited lifting power of aircraft. All of which seems to leave us with the one option which seems to fit all the requirements: ships.

Did the U.S. Navy, as Allende alleges, and as the evidence we have examined thus far seems to indicate, actually use the DE 173 to conduct such an experiment in electronic camouflage? Were the results as horrifying as he says they were? And did elements of the military-scientific establishment use the results of such tests as a basis for later research into possible methods of anti-gravity propulsion similar to the power source which Jessup and others since have inferred is used to power the UFO? Although this book has provided hitherto unpublished information which has gone a long way toward providing clues to the answers of those questions, the necessary positive proof seems as elusive as ever.

Can such proof be found? Probably not unless the government files on the project can be discovered and made public. And without knowledge of the military code name assigned to the project this would be difficult if not impossible. Any inquiry made to the Office of Naval Research on the topic generates at best nothing more than the curtly worded form letter, previously referred to, which flatly (and predictably) denies the whole thing. Concerning the Allende/Jessup affair, "The Office of Naval Research has never conducted an official study." With respect to the Philadelphia Experiment itself, "ONR has never conducted any investigations on invisibility, either in 1943 or at any other time." Pressed to an official conclusion, the Navy Department tends to chalk the whole thing up to nothing more than a poor attempt at "science fiction." Other government agencies tend to be even less cooperative.

Charles Berlitz, during research for his book *Without a Trace,* attempted discreet but thorough inquiry into the mystery at local key points involved. He was often coldly informed that the whole story was the result of someone having been carried away by his imagination. Even less productive was the response generated when he attempted to discuss the subject with officials of the Varo Corporation in Garland, Texas. "The company," he was told, "is not interested in discussing the subject with you or anyone else." In addition, he was advised that it would be useless to pursue the matter. As far as Varo was concerned, "All letters on the topic will go unanswered and all phone calls will be refused."

In spite of the official silence, one indication that something might have been going on can be found in the strange story of the famed mentalist and magician Joseph Dunninger. During the early phases of World War II, well before America's entry into that conflict, reports which apparently originated in Germany began to appear in the world press to the effect that the British had perfected some form of "secret varnish" which rendered their planes virtually invisible at night—even in the most powerful searchlights. Dunninger, who was certainly no stranger to the value of publicity, apparently read these stories and immediately saw them as the potential basis for a publicity coup. Consulting with several reporter friends upon whose confidence and advice he frequently relied, Dunninger cooked up a news release which he and his friends knew would be snapped up at once by the nation's press wires and splashed around the country. The scheme went off like clockwork, with the results as anticipated. Typical of these results is the following story, which appeared on page 5 of *The New York Times*, August 31, 1940:

Reports from Germany that the British are using a secret varnish on their bombing planes to make them invisible ... at night caused considerable comment and at least one novel explanation here yesterday.

Joseph Dunninger, magician and mind reader, holds...that their bombers are invisible because of a secret apparatus developed in England by Horace Goldin, world famous magician who died...a year ago.

The exact nature of the apparatus, said to make a plane in flight invisible either in day or night, was not disclosed by Mr. Dunninger, who asserted that he developed a similar apparatus in this country. Mr. Dunninger said he had demonstrated his apparatus, which made a model battleship invisible, at the United States Department [of the Navy] in Washington. He declined to explain the principle on which it worked.

With his apparatus, he said, he could make a battleship completely invisible. The equipment for doing this would weigh only about one-tenth as much as the ship. He said he could see no reason why it could not be applied to airplanes.

Literally besieged by newsmen, and in the height of his glory, Dunninger "reluctantly" arranged for a demonstration the next day to take place at the Ruxton Hotel in Washington, D.C. There, before a roomful of reporters, he patiently explained that since it was impossible to bring a battleship into the hotel, he would do the next best thing and go to work on a picture of one. True to promise, the picture promptly proceeded to vanish before their astonished eyes. According to Mrs. Chrystal Dunninger, who recalls the incident, the stunt created quite a sensation. "The reporters just didn't know what to make of it," she said.

On the next day a letter arrived from the Navy Department which expressed strong official interest in Dunninger's "discovery." The letter requested that additional information be provided and that a demonstration be arranged "as soon as possible." According to Mrs. Dunninger, "The whole thing was a stunt and there really was no apparatus. And that was the end of it."

Except that it wasn't; for when Dunninger failed to respond to the letter, the Navy sent two officers to discuss the affair with him. The upshot of this unanticipated turn of events was that Dunninger was obliged to admit the whole thing was a hoax. In the process of doing so, however, he confided that he did have certain ideas about how Navy ships might be made invisible through the use of an artificial mirage induced by manipulating the sun's rays. Requested to submit his plan in writing, Dunninger finally did so after Pearl Harbor. The Navy's response was to immediately oblige him to sign a document swearing him to a "complete, total and permanent silence" in regards to the whole matter. What Dunninger actually submitted and what the Navy subsequently did with it remains unknown.

Another indication of the U.S. Navy's intense interest in the late 1930s and early 1940s in the shipboard use of strong magnetic fields, at least as an anti-mine measure, comes in a book entitled *Magnets, the Education of a Physicist* (Cambridge, 1956) by the late prominent magnetic physicist Dr. Francis Bitter, founder of the Magnet Laboratory at MIT. Bitter, while failing to go deeply into technical details, nonetheless devotes an entire chapter of his book to telling the story of how the technique of electromagnetic ship degaussing was developed as a countermeasure to the highly dangerous magnetic mines which had been invented by the Germans during the 1930s.

According to an account by C. M. Fowler and T. Erber (*Francis Bitter, Selected Papers and Commentaries,* Cambridge, 1969), Dr. Bitter's research "eventually led to elaborate countermeasures *designed to make shipping magnetically 'invisible'* to the ... [German] mines." Of course, invisibility to the sensing mechanisms of undersea mines and invisibility to human sight are two entirely different things, but we are nonetheless prompted to wonder whether Bitter's research into this area of "magnetic invisibility" might not have been the beginnings of a more complex project aimed at achieving the total invisibility Allende describes.

There can be no doubt that relatively immense magnets and the enormous magnetic fields associated with them were in use during these early experiments. Dr. Bitter himself, writing in *Magnets,* states that he witnessed "a relatively large ship carrying a very strong magnet weighing *many, many tons*. This was a bar magnet going from the bow of the ship, usually near the top deck, way aft. This bar magnet had coils wound around it which passed a current produced by big motor generators."

Interested to discover whether these early degaussing experiments may in fact have been forerunners of the far more complicated Philadelphia Experiment, Moore attempted an investigative ploy with another scientist known to have been heavily involved in the Navy's early degaussing efforts. Having previously written a brief account of that scientist's life as part of a projected magazine article, he hit upon the idea of trying to determine whether he knew anything about Allende's ship experiment by arranging to have him edit and approve a draft of that article, and then loading the draft with a specially prepared paragraph before submitting it to him. Thus, the draft manuscript which he received contained the following "planted" paragraph:

The war saw [the scientist in question] almost continuously involved as a physicist with . . . the National Defense Research Committee. One of these projects involved exposing first models and later a U.S. Navy ship to an intense electromagnetic field in order to observe the effects of the field on material objects. The field was produced through the use of Navy ship degaussing equipment utilizing the principle of resonance so as to produce extreme results. Some of the accounts of this project are more spectacular than others (at least one source claims that the experiment produced extreme physical reactions upon exposed crew members), but whatever the results, the project was discontinued in late 1943.

The object of this ruse, of course, was to observe this man's reaction to the planted material by watching what he did with it in the editing process. The surprise came with the return of the edited document. As requested the scientist had indeed penciled in numerous suggestions, corrections, additions, and deletions... *but he had allowed to stand without change or comment the entire test paragraph!* Only two conclusions were possible: Either the man had committed a gross oversight in his editing, or the experiment actually did occur as described! The cover letter which came with the manuscript seemed to clinch it. "As to the draft of your article," it said, the information "appears to be essentially correct."

But what about these side effects? One of the strangest and most disturbing aspects of Allende's tale is his descriptions of the extreme physical and mental side effects of the invisibility experiment on the ship's crew. In fact, it is this utterly fantastic quality which has led many of the story's detractors to conclude that the Allende letters represent nothing more than a grotesque expression of insanity. After all, they point out, if human exposure to electrical force fields could cause such things as invisibility and insanity, then we all should have long since become invisible or insane. The other side of the argument is represented by those who contend that such effects did occur and that the Navy's subsequent fear and embarrassment is the cause for the continued secrecy.

Some interesting new light was shed on this controversy in late 1976 with the release of a previously Top Secret government intelligence report which deals with recent Soviet studies of the effects of high-frequency electromagnetic force fields upon the human organism. An unsettling aspect about the report is that it speaks of an unsettling number of changes in brain function and body chemistry which the Russians have discovered can be directly induced by exposure to electromagnetic fields. Such fields, it goes on to say, were found to have "great potential for development into a system for disorienting and disrupting the behavior patterns of . . . personnel." Included among the noted effects were "severe neurological and cardiovascular [circulatory] disturbances, dizziness, forgetfulness, lack of concentration, and alternating states of anxiety and depression."

The main difference between these disturbing effects and the more horrifying ones which Allende alleges were experienced by the hapless crew of the Navy's experimental vessel is that the Russians supposedly produced the effects noted by using electromagnetic field radiation of *low intensity*. The fields which would have been produced by anything approaching the magnitude of the so-called Philadelphia Experiment would undoubtedly have been of a tremendously higher energy level.

Two other seeming confirmations that such an experiment did indeed take place also arrived in the form of letters—both by way of Dr. Reilly H. Crabb of BSRF (see Chapter 2). The first was a copy of a letter from a Navy man to Dr. Crabb in which the writer, a man named Griffin, stated that he had heard of Crabb's interest in the Jessup/Allende disappearing-ship experiment and was writing because he thought he might be able to add something. He went on to say that some years before while stationed on the island of Cyprus in the Mediterranean, he had encountered the old DE 173, then serving in the Greek navy under the name *Léon*. According to Griffin's letter, during this ship's stay in port a certain individual had pointed out to him that this was the ship which the Americans had tried to make invisible during World War II. Crabb says the reason he took particular notice of this letter was that it was the first time he had ever run across anyone who claimed to know the name of the ship which had been involved in the invisibility experiments mentioned in the Allende letters. Allende himself had named only the S.S. *Furuseth* in his letters to Jessup, and in fact only many years later disclosed that the name of the experimental ship was the DE 173! If Griffin's informant didn't get his information from Allende, then where *did* he get it?

The second letter was even more interesting. This one came in the form of an inquiry from a Mr. Shoumake to Dr. Crabb. After an initial paragraph asking Crabb for information regarding BSRF publications and membership, Shoumake dropped the following bombshell: "During the 1950s," he wrote, "my uncle, a retired naval warrant officer, related specifics of events classified as Top Secret at the Philadelphia Navy Yard. Through a friend I obtained a copy of your publication on M. K. Jessup and the Allende letters which filled in many of the voids remaining..."

Unfortunately, although Moore (with the approval of Mr. Crabb) has made repeated attempts to contact Mr. Shoumake concerning this intriguing statement, nothing further has ever turned up regarding either Mr. Shoumake or his most interesting uncle. Hoax? Perhaps... and again, perhaps not.

An unusual aspect of researching the Philadelphia Experiment is the variety of testimony that comes from individuals in widely separated places, testimony contributing sometimes seemingly unimportant details that, when linked in time and place, provide an occasionally startling corroboration. Frequently the name or address of an informant is unavailable, because so much time has elapsed since the incident, or an informant feels revealing his identity would work against him.

An unusual report was unexpectedly received by Patrick Macey, an electronic construction specialist and researcher, while he was working on contract in Los Angeles in the summer of 1977. He and another contract worker (Macey remembers him only as "Jim") were discussing UFOs and how much the government was "covering up."

"I had an unusual experience during WW II, while I was in the Navy," said Jim, "not with UFOs, but something pretty mysterious. I was a guard for classified audiovisual material, and in late 1945 I was in a position, while on duty in Washington, to see part of a film viewed by a lot of Navy brass, pertaining to an experiment done at sea. I remember only part of the film, as my security duties did not permit me to sit and look at it like the others. I didn't know what was going on in the film, since it was without commentary. I do remember that it concerned three ships. When they rolled the film, it showed two other ships feeding some sort of energy into the central ship. I thought it was sound waves, but I didn't know, since I, naturally, wasn't in on the briefing.

"After a time the central ship, a destroyer, disappeared slowly into a transparent fog until all that could be seen was an imprint of that ship in the water. Then, when the field, or whatever it was, was turned off, the ship reappeared slowly out of thin fog.

"Apparently that was the end of the film, and I overheard some of the men in the room discussing it. Some thought that the field had been left on too long and that that had caused the problems that some of the crew members were having.

"Somebody mentioned an incident where one of the crewmen apparently disappeared while drinking in a bar. Somebody else commented that the crew were 'still not in their right minds, and may never be.' There were also some references to some of the crew having vanished permanently. At that point the conversation was carried on outside of my hearing."

This corroborative (although presently unverifiable) account is pertinent in that it alludes directly to the information contained in Allende's startling letters, and also to reported newspaper accounts (see following pages). One may wonder why, if such a film existed, it would have been shown in 1945? A logical explanation would be that, after the conclusion of WW II, certain projects abandoned or interrupted during the war were reviewed for assessment or revival. Perhaps the Philadelphia Experiment was one of these.

The names of several scientists have come up in connection with the revival of such a project. Two government-employed scientists named Charlesworth and Carroll were reportedly responsible for installing the auxiliary equipment on the DE-173 and participated in the experiment, noting the neuronal damage "due to diatheric" effect because of the magnetic oscillation of the magnetic field."

When the project was interrupted, partially because of the effect on the crew and possibly also because of the imminent success of another highly classified project—the atom bomb—Charlesworth nevertheless maintained his interest in it. At the close of World War II he is alleged to have suggested to his superiors that the project be reconsidered—under his direction—and this may have been the occasion for the showing of the classified film described above.

Then there is the matter of those elusive newspaper articles—the bits of evidence which, if they could be found and verified, might provide an answer to the entire mystery. According to Allende, there were two of these. The first, which he says he saw in a Philadelphia newspaper, concerned a barroom incident during which several sailors, supposedly on shore leave from the experimental ship, were alleged to have exhibited strange effects caused by the force fields used in the experiments. The second, which may have been in a Norfolk-area newspaper, dealt with a ship's sudden appearance and subsequent disappearance from the Norfolk Harbor area (teleportation?).

In addition, several people came forward during the course of the authors' investigations who claimed to remember the same or similar press articles and even magazine coverage of these matters. One of the most frequently mentioned is one said to have appeared in the pages of the old *New York World-Telegram* between early 1940 and late 1944. Reilly Crabb maintains that an investigator telephoned him some years ago and said he'd spent weeks searching the entire *World-Telegram* file at the New York Public Library but was unable to find it. The closest we got, he said, was the interesting discovery that there were entire pages missing from several of the papers issued during that time period.

Other sources have mentioned *Life* and *Male* magazines and the *New York World-Telegram* as having published articles dealing with the project. One such source is an obscure and rather bizarre tract entitled "The Hefferlin Manuscript" which apparently antedates the Allende letters. Mentioned therein is an illustrated *Life* article supposedly from sometime during the 1940s which allegedly dealt with experiments in invisibility conducted by Hungarian scientists during the early days of World War II. Although the account is unclear about whether those took place in Hungary or the United States, it is interesting to note that Dr. John von Neumann, the man named by Dr. Rinehart as one of the early prime movers in the invisibility project, was born in Budapest in 1903.

Through all of this, however, the key article still seems to be the one Allende claims to have seen in 1943. Although many claim to have searched for this bit of evidence over the years, no one, up to the present time, has been able to report even the slightest success—much to the satisfaction of the story's detractors. Now, with the writing of this book, it is finally possible to announce what appears to be a breakthrough in this all-important area of the mystery. In a secure safety deposit box there exists a photocopy of a newspaper clipping which was received from an anonymous source and which, up to now, has managed to survive all efforts to discredit its authenticity. The clipping, undated and without identification as to newspaper of origin, reads as follows:

Strange Circumstances
Surround Tavern Brawl

Several city police officers responding to a call to aid members of the Navy Shore Patrol in breaking up a tavern brawl near the U.S. Navy docks here last night got something of a surprise when they arrived on the scene to find the place empty of customers. According to a pair of very nervous waitresses, the Shore Patrol had arrived first and cleared the place out—but not before two of the sailors involved allegedly did a disappearing act. "They just sort of vanished into thin air . . . right there," reported one of the frightened hostesses, "and I ain't been drinking either!" At that point, according to her account, the Shore Patrol proceeded to hustle everybody out of the place in short order.

A subsequent chat with the local police precinct left no doubts as to the fact that some sort of general brawl had indeed occurred in the vicinity of the dockyards at about eleven o'clock last night, but neither confirmation nor denial of the stranger aspects of the story could be immediately obtained. One reported witness succinctly summed up the affair by dismissing it as nothing more than "a lot of hooey from them daffy dames down there," who, he went on to say, were probably just looking for some free publicity.

Damage to the tavern was estimated to be in the vicinity of six hundred dollars.

Little else can be said about the clipping itself. Anything approaching a proper analysis of the clipping is impossible, since only a photocopy is available. Upon close examination, however, the one possibly significant fact that emerges is that the column width is a bit greater than was used by any of the Philadelphia dailies in the 1940s. This suggests that the article may have originated in a local or regional newspaper in the Philadelphia area rather than in one of the metropolitan papers. Another possibility is that it may be from a Camden or Newark paper—a supposition which is partially supported by the fact that the Camden newspaper had something of a reputation for sloppy typography during the war years.

As to the source of the photocopy itself, the authors have made several attempts to pin this one down—even going so far as to resort to a bit of "trickery" on their own in an attempt to smoke out the source. All, however, to no avail. At the time of this writing, the best guess is that it was sent anonymously in answer to one of our inquiries by the same elusive person who related to Reilly Crabb that his uncle was "a retired naval warrant officer." This, of course, is strictly conjecture and is based on nothing more than the fact that the envelope that the clipping arrived in was postmarked from the same city that the letter to Crabb had come from. Until the article itself can be actually verified either by identifying the source of the photocopy or by discovering the name and date of the newspaper in which the article originally appeared, its existence will continue to remain a puzzle.

Within the last several years Charles Berlitz has encountered, during lectures on the Bermuda Triangle given in many cities in America and Europe, a number of corroborative reports from members of the lecture audiences about the Philadelphia Experiment, even though only the briefest reference had been made to it in the lecture. Such reports, given from the audience, were especially numerous in cities like Philadelphia, Trenton, Baltimore, and Washington. In many cases, individuals would claim to have been employed at the Philadelphia Navy Yard at the time, or to have learned of the unusual behavior of the DE-173 while on convoy duty, to have known one or several of the seamen involved in the experiment, or to have heard at the time of the disappearing fighters in the Seamen's Lounge. In each case, however, the person in question evinced a firm determination not to give his or her name, sometimes citing the high security classification then in force and sometimes mentioning possible danger to themselves.

One unusually specific corroboration came from a seaman who claimed to have been on board during the dockside experiment in the Philadelphia Navy Yard and who, since the incident, has suffered a number of premature heart attacks.

Victor Silverman, now living in Pennsylvania and still mindful of wartime security regulations and afraid of possible consequences, got in touch with the authors through a third party when he first heard about the publication of a book about the DE-173. He speaks from personal experience: "I was on that ship at the time of the experiment."

At the outbreak of WWII Silverman enlisted in the Navy. He, along with about 40 others, was destined to become part of a special secret Naval experimental project involving a destroyer escort vessel and a process which he could identify only as "degaussing". On board the vessel, Silverman noted that there was "enough radar equipment on the ship to fill a battleship" including "an extra mast" which was "rigged out like a Christmas tree" with what appeared to be antenna-like structures.

At one point during the preparation for the experiment, Silverman remembers seeing a civilian on board and said to a shipmate: "That guy could use a haircut." To his amazement he later discovered that the man had been Albert Einstein.

Silverman was given the rating of Engineer, First Class, and, according to his account, was one of three seamen who knew where the switches were that started the operation. He also related that a special series of electrical cables had been laid from a nearby power house to the ship. When the order was given and the switches thrown, "the resulting whine was almost unbearable."

On another occasion Silverman quite unexpectedly found himself in a deep fog and his first thought was that he had somehow been blown off the ship. As he stood there trying to comprehend what had happened, and looking for his ship, he watched indistinct figures in motion whom he could not identify as sailors and some other shapes "that did not seem to belong on the dock, if that is where I was."

Suddenly the deep fog "flashed off," leaving Silverman in a very confused state and wondering, "what in the world I was doing in Norfolk." He said he had recognized the place as Norfolk "because I had been there before to the ship's other dock there." Then, just as suddenly, the green fog returned; it lifted again and Silverman found himself back at dockside in the Philadelphia Navy Yard. "For a long time afterwards," he related, "I was left wondering whether or not I hadn't lost my mind for those few brief moments. I still don't know exactly what happened to me or to the other men who were there."

Also very important is the fact that Silverman was able to recall the "barroom brawl" incident which occurred shortly after this episode. "When the Captain got word of this, he ordered everyone back aboard ship as fast as we could get there. We immediately put off from shore and stood out in the river all night until he got it straightened out."

With respect to the newspaper article which appears on pages 44–45, Silverman commented only that his recollection was that "the damage amounted to only $300." "Of course," he said, "that could have been $300 for each of the two men who were involved. I really never thought about it in that way before." As for the names of the two men, "one of them was Wilkens. The other one had a Polish or Ukrainian name that began with a D."

On another occasion, Silverman recalls passing the ship's radar shack and running head-long into a party of three civilians who were just coming out of it. He remembers that one of them said to the others something about "the experiment having been a great success." When these three men left the ship they were carrying between them "a black leather covered box about the size of a footlocker."

Shortly after the experiments, one of which took place at sea and may have been witnessed by Allende, Silverman spent six months in Bethesda Naval Hospital, three of them in what was known as "a quiet area." While he was in the hospital an admiral—he thinks it was Admiral Bowen—came to visit him and others who had been hospitalized after the experiment. Silverman has since suffered a series of three heart attacks which he feels may be directly related to his experiences in Philadelphia.

Did anyone on shore see the unexpected apparition of a destroyer escort in Norfolk harbor, as the DE-173 allegedly slipped in space—and time? Tony Wells, now living in Southhampton, England, writes about five British merchant seamen who, in 1943, were waiting in Norfolk for berths on Liberty Ships destined to go to England. One day, looking at the harbor from the dock, they were understandably amazed to see a sea-level cloud suddenly form in the harbor, and almost immediately dissipate, leaving a destroyer escort in full view, which stayed but a few moments before it was covered by a cloud and vanished again. While the bemused seamen were wondering whether what they thought they had seen was real, the whole area was cleared by Naval Security and Shore Patrol personnel. The seamen decided that perhaps in the best interests of getting back to England as soon as possible, it was best not to talk about "whatever sort of projection or camouflage the Yanks were up to," and so only recently corroborated their chance sighting of the elusive DE-173.

A rather convincing indication that an experiment similar to the reputed Philadelphia Experiment took place more or less as reported and was the subject of a secret memorandum read to certain officers and crews from the Secretary of the Navy comes from Frederick Tracy, a Navy WWII veteran who served on three ships, one of which was the U.S.S. *Antietam,* CV-36.

Tracy had heard about the Philadelphia Experiment from a shipmate, Fireman First Class D. J. Myers, in 1944 when their ship was in drydock in Philadelphia. Myers pointed out a dock and said, "See that dock over there? That's the dock a ship once disappeared at." Myers thereupon told Tracy the story. When he was finished, Tracy said, "I don't believe you." To which Myers replied, "I didn't think you would."

The next year, however, when the *Antietam* went into the Philadelphia Navy Yard for degaussing, scuttlebutt started among the crew about the possibility of another "Philadelphia Experiment." To offset this, the Captain of the *Antietam* called the crew to quarters and explained that the matter at hand was simply ordinary degaussing with no danger to the crew. At the same time he read a memorandum from the Secretary of the Navy to everyone standing at quarters. While he was reading, Tracy caught the eye of Myers who, standing in a rear rank, was radiating a smug "didn't I tell you so" attitude.

According to Tracy's recollection, the memo stated that the incident happened on October 28, 1943, and concerned a PC (patrol craft) which vanished during a degaussing experiment, then appeared off Norfolk and returned to the dock in the Philadelphia Navy Yard with some crew members missing and others affected mentally and physically. Although some of the officers and men were inclined to treat the matter as a joke, the captain stressed that to "mention or talk about this incident outside the confines of the vessel would constitute an act of treason."

The reading of the memo at quarters was entered into the log of the *Antietam* during May 1945. The captain who made the announcement was Captain Teague; the Executive Officer was Commander Haywood (who hung himself in the wardroom at about the time of the war's end).

Tracy believes that there was a change in the names of the subject ships: from the Navy ship *Yarmawa* to the Coast Guard *Eldridge,* and vice versa, with a view to further covering the trail of the experiment. As for the crew, Tracy says, "The only thing I ever heard about the crew of the *Eldridge* was that they were kept at Bethesda Naval Hospital out of communication with everybody for the remainder of the war."

Reports continue to come in. A rather startling one concerns a woman who allegedly had an affair with one of the seamen from the DE-173. He began to suffer adverse effects from the field, marked by "strange symptoms," and was rushed off to Bethesda Hospital by the Navy. The woman, considerably affected by this incident, became despondent and shortly afterward lost her life in a "freak accident."

Still another problem which continues to plague this whole mystery is that strange circumstances relating to Morris Jessup's death continue to turn up. Was his death really the suicide it appears to have been, or was he murdered because he knew too much? Recently additional evidence has come to light.

The first bit of evidence comes by way of Mrs. Anna Genslinger of Miami, who, along with a police lieutenant friend of hers, has obtained access to the Dade County, Florida, medical examiner's files on the Jessup case. It was in these records that she discovered that at the time of his death Jessup's blood was virtually saturated with what would normally be considered more than a lethal amount of alcohol. According to Mrs. Genslinger, Jessup was also taking a medication at the time which, when combined with such an amount of alcohol, could have been immediately fatal or at least would have been far more than enough to incapacitate him totally.

He would have been completely unable even to get in a car under his own power, much less drive one several miles to a county park, write a suicide note, and then attach a hose to the exhaust pipe of the vehicle. Furthermore, no autopsy was ever performed on the body—an unusual occurrence in a suicide case. Of course, none of this constitutes conclusive evidence for murder, but it is nonetheless of interest.

Equally interesting is a comment made to the author by James R. Wolfe, a freelance writer and researcher who had himself spent some time looking into the Allende mystery. Wolfe had started to write a book on the topic when he became a mystery himself by turning up missing before it was completed. Even stranger is the fact that it was Wolfe's disappearance which led to the discovery of the additional evidence presented in the next chapter. Before his disappearance, however, Wolfe had exchanged with the authors useful bits and pieces of information. In discussing Jessup's possible murder, Wolfe, a former Navy man, indicated that he didn't believe it at first but later became convinced. He went on to say that "the big reason for the continued secret classification on the Philadelphia Experiment is not the damage that knowledge of it would do the Navy—but the damage it would do to the image of *an individual*." That individual, according to Wolfe, carried more than enough clout not only to arrange for Jessup's murder, but to see to it that the job was neatly done. He did not, however, identify the individual he had in mind.

Looking in other directions, perhaps yet another hint as to the reason for the continued secrecy has already been provided to us by one of Charles Berlitz' informants. This informant, who emphatically declined to be named, confided to Berlitz that he had seen highly classified documents in the Navy files in Washington, D.C., which indicated that at least some phases of the experiments are *still* in progress.

In addition, scientific units in private universities, some possibly funded by the government, are reported to be pursuing research in magnetic teleportation, with the attendant invisibility as part of the experiment. Some recent reports place such experimentation as having taken place at Stanford University Research Facility at Menlo Park, Palo Alto, California, and at M.I.T. in Boston. However, in the words of one informant—M. Akers, a psychologist in San Jose, California—such magnetic experiments "are frowned upon because they have detrimental effects on the researchers conducting the experiments."

Did the Philadelphia Experiment really happen? Is it perhaps still happening? The final chapter to this unofficial investigation provides the strangest piece of the puzzle yet uncovered.

CHAPTER 12

The Circle
Closes

The first chapter in this book dealt with an unusual corroboration of the Philadelphia Experiment from an unexpected encounter in a park in Colorado Springs. To a neutral investigator, of course, this account might be considered suspect because of the statement that "some of the men involved in the ship experiment had passed into another world and had seen and talked to strange alien beings." It is certainly easy to doubt that, in the course of their work with force fields and their attempts to create radar invisibility, the U.S. Navy inadvertently stumbled upon a pathway to another world, or that by means of the so-called Philadelphia Experiment our government actually achieved contact with an alien civilization as far back as mid-WW II and has *maintained* this contact right up to the present day on a top-secret basis. Nevertheless, if this *were* the case, it could explain the official curtain of silence on a great many topics, not the least of which would be UFOs. But how to prove it? Surely the unsupported word of an unidentified man in a Colorado park can hardly be taken as conclusive proof. Where to go from there short of finding the man himself?—an unlikely occurrence in any event. Even presuming he could be traced, what could he possibly have to offer beyond the story he has already told?

If we are to attempt to substantiate such a bizarre claim, it would have to be through another witness—someone totally unrelated to the Davis/Huse incident who could relate the same or highly similar facts. If such a source could be discovered, then at least a measure of credibility would be added to what is up to this point a somewhat incredible story. But can such a source be found?

Recent evidence indicates that another source has surfaced. The coincidences that led to its discovery are almost as startling as the story itself and ultimately lead us back to researcher and writer James R. Wolfe, mentioned in the previous chapter as having arrived at a few conclusions of his own with respect to the connection between Allende and the Philadelphia Experiment.

Moore's report follows:

In February 1978, some months after my last contact with Wolfe, I began hearing rumors from various sources that Wolfe had disappeared. One of these tips came to me by way of Charles Berlitz, who said he had heard the story from a business contact in the publishing world. Curious, but busy with other matters at the time, I failed to follow up on the matter right away, and when I finally did take time to write to Wolfe, my letter came back a few days later marked "Not at this address." I thought it strange, but I again put off taking any further action until I had more time to look into it.

A series of extraordinary coincidences now took place. Early in May 1978 I received a telephone call from a Michelle Alberti, who identified herself as secretary of CUFORN, Inc., a Canadian psychic research group in Willowdale, Ontario. She explained that during her group's investigation of the Philadelphia Experiment she had learned of a James R. Wolfe who was said to have information on the matter. While trying to locate Wolfe, she was dismayed to discover that he had "disappeared." Further inquiries turned up "evidence" that Wolfe was dead. Immediately suspecting the possibility of another "Jessup-type incident," she called Gray Barker in Clarksburg, West Virginia, to see what he knew. During the course of the conversation, Barker gave her my name as someone who was not only very deeply involved in investigating the Philadelphia Experiment but had been in regular contact with Wolfe. "This is why I called you," she said. "Is there anything you can tell me about the circumstances surrounding Wolfe's death?"

After recovering from my initial shock I wasn't able to be very helpful. I admitted that I had heard rumors that Wolfe was missing, but that I knew nothing definite on the subject. "As a matter of fact," I said, "your telling me that he is dead comes as quite a shock to me." I told her I would get back to her if anything turned up. As of the time of this writing, the matter of the Wolfe disappearance and rumored death is still something of a mystery; first, concerning why and how the false report was disseminated and, secondly, the question of where Wolfe is now. As Michelle and I continued talking, I asked her how she had become interested in the Philadelphia Experiment. "It came," she said, "as the result of our investigation of a close encounter of the third kind here in Canada." The story was as follows: Late in the evening on Tuesday, October 7, 1975, Robert Suffern, a twenty-seven-year-old carpenter from rural Bracebridge, Ontario, received a call from his sister, who lives down the road, asking him to investigate a strange glow that seemed to be coming from a nearby barn. Suffern drove to the barn, took a quick look around, and not seeing anything out of the ordinary, was proceeding to his sister's house when he was startled to see a darkened saucer-shaped object about 12 to 14 feet in diameter squatting on the graveled road directly ahead of him.

"I was scared," he later recounted to a *Toronto Sun* reporter. "It was right there in front of me with no lights and no signs of life." His car hadn't quite come to a full stop, he said, when the object "went straight up in the air and out of sight."

According to Suffern's story, he had no sooner managed to turn his car around and head for home when a strange, 4-foot-tall humanlike creature with "very wide shoulders which were out of proportion to his body" and wearing a silver-gray suit and a globe-type helmet walked out into the road right in front of his car. Suffern slammed on the brakes, skidding on the loose gravel, and came within inches of colliding with the creature, who promptly dodged out of the way, ran to the side of the road, jumped a fence, and disappeared into a field. According to the account Suffern gave to the *Sun* reporter, when the figure "got to the fence, he put his hands on a post and went over it with no effort at all. It was like he was weightless."

Badly shaken by this encounter, Suffern finally succeeded in driving home, only to discover when he looked out the window of his house that the UFO had returned, this time flying slowly close over the road. At that moment, it flew around an electric pole and again disappeared, seemingly going straight up into the night sky.

Neither relatives, close friends, nor the reporters, investigators, and plain curious who descended on his farmhouse over the next several weeks could dislodge him from his story.

"I know what I saw," he said. "But I don't care if I ever see that creature again."

Of course, if the story ended at this point, it would be nothing more than another addition to an ever growing list of mysterious and difficult-to-verify close-encounter cases in recent years. But there was more. On July 15, 1976, some nine months after the Bracebridge incident, Harry Tokarz, a CUFORN investigator, along with a freelance movie maker, was "tracking down several UFO reports throughout Ontario" for possible inclusion in the documentary film *UFO-the Canadian Perspective*. Finding themselves in the Bracebridge area, they decided to pay a visit to Suffern and perhaps get a useful follow-up on his 1975 encounter.

Neither Suffern, who is described by Tokarz, as "an individual who carefully measures his thoughts," nor his wife, "a home-bred country girl, quick to air her views," was especially anxious to discuss UFOs—no real surprise, considering the pressure this couple had undergone following the October incident. It took a promise of no equipment and the investigator's word that all they were really interested in was "obtaining any new details which may not have emerged during the . . . investigations of the previous year before they were willing to talk at all." The result was a five-hour interview of the most interesting sort.

"Once the Sufferns eased into the topic of UFOs, a couple of intriguing facts came to light. First, both Suffern and his wife 'believed' themselves to be totally enlightened on UFOs without necessarily attaching a lot of importance to the subject. Secondly, we discovered that they had not discussed the following matter with *anyone* previously."

Actually, the only reason these "startling revelations" appear to have been made at all by the Sufferns is because of an apparent slip of the tongue on the part of Mrs. Suffern during the interview.

Quoting from Tokarz's own account, which appeared in the May 1977 issue of CUFORN's journal, *The Pulse Analyzer:*

Once we became alerted to the situation, Suffern dropped his guard and decided to confide in us. Reluctant at first, he soon began discussing the situation seriously. He seemed genuinely concerned with our own particular concern in this matter. The less we pried, the more he revealed....

On December 12, 1975, after the Sufferns were beginning to feel some semblance of order again (their farm was literally swamped for weeks by roving bands of curiosity seekers) three men were delivered to their home in an Ontario Provincial Police cruiser. The appointment had been prearranged in November. These officials arrived in full uniform, bearing impressive credentials and representing themselves as the TOP BRASS from the Canadian Forces in Ottawa, the United States Air Force, Pentagon, and from the Office of Naval Intelligence. Suffern, previously perturbed about the nature of his UFO encounter, claimed that ALL his questions were answered POINT BLANK and with NO HESITATIONS by these three helpful gentlemen. They "opened the books" to him and gave him the answers to the WHERE FROM, the What and the Why. They implied that the U.S. and Canadian governments have known all about UFOs since 1943 and have in fact been cooperating with the ALIENS in some unknown capacity since then!

As if this wasn't enough to swallow in one gulp, the military "knows-it-alls" threw us yet another curve when they made a formal APOLOGY to Suffern for the unfortunate incident of Oct. 7. They claimed it was a MISTAKE!! To which Suffern immediately thought out loud that it must have been a super-secret military craft. No, they claimed. It was a malfunction in the saucer that brought the craft down, complete with aliens, on his property. Mrs. Suffern found all this quite impossible to accept, but when she quizzed them, the officers actually came up with the exact time of the landing—to the minute—a small detail that only the Sufferns knew and had not conveyed to anyone. They have had three different UFO sightings over their property, only the last of which they reported, and *again* the times and dates were duly related to them by the knowledgeable trio. The enlightened agents, carrying a battery of books and data (complete with gun camera photos of UFOs), again emphasized that the landing was an ACCIDENT and should not have occurred....

...Further along we learned that the military still refer to UFO occupants as "humanoids." Contact was apparently made in 1943 (reputedly through an accident that occurred during a naval experiment involving radar invisibility) and now our forces are aware of the aliens' movements on this planet....

...Suffern adamantly insisted that all his questions about the craft and the occupant were answered "to his satisfaction" despite the fact that (many) civilian investigators have visited him and offered alternate hypotheses to clear up the mystery for him. Many came close but none answered him with the same "degree of accuracy"...

...The critical key to Suffern's encounter is the fact that he had a "near miss" car situation with a physical entity, dressed in a one-piece silver suit and short in stature. If contact *indeed* has taken place then there could have been serious repercussions, had he actually run the being down. This could account for the military's intervention and unusual frankness....

The Sufferns remained firm in their statement that all three military personnel answered all their questions with uncanny pre-

cision and immediately. Suffern himself claims
that he knows the identities of these three men
and can prove that they were not imposters. He
also denies he is bound by the Canadian Secrets
Act and claims that his only motive for keeping
the details secret is for the "moral reason" of
simply wanting to keep his part of the bargain
by complying with the "government's wishes."

One further item of interest is the apparent
existence of certain evidence of an undisclosed
nature which the CUFORN investigator claims
to have turned up that indicates the Canadian
and U.S. authorities conducted an extensive
medical and psychological check on the Sufferns
before their secret meeting with them in December—possibly for the purpose of trying to
predict how the Sufferns would react to the dis-
closures.

This account, fantastic as it may seem, nevertheless appears to be significantly connected to
the revelations made to Davis and Huse by the
man in the park in Colorado Springs some years
earlier. Could Suffern have heard of this incident and expanded upon it in order to create
his own version of the story? The reference to
"aliens' contact in 1943," and the perplexing
appearance of an American Navy officer from
the Office of Naval Intelligence—an agency not
normally having any connection whatsoever to
UFO investigations—become more understandable when we place them in the context of possible interest on the part of the Office of Naval
Intelligence and/or Office of Naval Research, in

keeping tabs on continuing developments related to the effects or repercussions of the officially "non-existent" Philadelphia Experiment.

Any reference to UFOs or "aliens," of course, tends to cast doubt on the authenticity of any mystery or theory about it. Nevertheless, UFOs seem to be an actuality, whatever their source, identity, or purpose, and those technicians concerned with space—astronomers, astronauts, physicists, and cosmologists—are often considerably less skeptical about unidentified flying objects than government agencies. Some scientists, neither struggling to prove or disprove the presence of UFOs in our skies, speculate on why they manifest themselves in certain places at certain times.

Professor Stan Friedman, a nuclear physicist of Hayward, California, has speculated that the reason that alien intelligences may have been attracted to the Philadelphia Experiment might be because of large concentrations of electromagnetic "oversplash" produced by the experiment itself. Professor Friedman, who has personally investigated a number of other cases in which UFOs have reportedly appeared in uninvited response to electromagnetic experimentation, theorizes that, if aliens are observing our world, they would be likely to have a functional electromagnetic map, and, when bright spots or points appeared, not accounted for on their grid, they would naturally investigate its source.

The search for information about the Philadelphia Experiment has led to many places, to many individuals, and to numberless files, records, and many dead-ends. But it has occasionally uncovered information neither looked for nor suspected, notably references to extraterrestrial (or interdimensional) entities. Presumably, if a vessel *could* be projected into another space or energy continuum through mistake or design, it might also be possible that its occupants could encounter entities on the other side of the curtain of invisibility shrouding contiguous but nontangent worlds. It is intriguing to conceive the possibility that an experiment sponsored by the U.S. Navy may have accidentally managed to pass through a doorway into another world more than thirty-five years ago and that the experiment and the results have been kept a closely guarded secret ever since.

Irrespective of the truth of this assumption, we are still left with the perplexing question of what possible motive the Canadian-U.S. military intelligence establishment could have for revealing such information to the Sufferns. There might be several distinct possibilities: (1) It's all part of a scheme designed to introduce the public to the truth bit by bit over a long period of time—beginning with obscure sources and graduating later on to more official ones. (2) The whole thing is an intelligence-agency ploy of some sort designed either to test the psychological impact that such a story would have on certain "target" individuals or to becloud further an already foggy issue. (3) There actually was an unavoidable and nearly tragic mishap and representatives of two governments had received orders from higher headquarters (presumably of this world) to "apologize" for it.

Beside these possibilities, of course, there may be still others connected with motives and forces at present too indistinct for us to be able to give them form.

This, in a certain sense, has been a notable characteristic of the alleged Philadelphia Experiment. But something happened at the Philadelphia Navy Yard in 1943 that left distinct traces in popular legend, in books, in newspaper articles, in documents, and in men's minds.

It would, of course, not be the first occasion that a scientific breakthrough happened before its time, and was abandoned because of unforeseen aftereffects or simply because the need for the experiment had been obviated by something more pressing—as in this case of a successful atom bomb weighed against a hard-to-control invisibility experiment that included interdimensional ramifications.

An opinion from an accredited scientist, Dr. James W. Moffet, a physicist at the University of Toronto, is worth considering here. Asked whether such a thing as the Philadelphia Experiment could happen, he replied that on a cosmic or astrophysical level such phenomena occur "all the time." He said he was used to working with problems of this nature as a matter of course, although they are strictly limited to large amounts of energy and large astrophysical bodies. In his words, "To bring such a phenomenon down to the level of the earth under the conditions present here does not seem to fit into the scope of present theory.

"However, you must remember when Einstein promulgated his relativity theory in 1905 he was doing so in regard to large bodies at astrophysical levels and it never occurred to him that his theories might apply to actions taking place between single atoms. When it became evident in the 1930s that it would be possible to split the atom at a controlled level it became necessary to reexamine the relativity theory to see whether it would account for such a possibility. It did—and the result served to further strengthen the theory itself. The same thing *could* be true of the Unified Field Theory—which now seems to be applicable on the astrophysical level but which *may* have further applications which science has not yet discovered.

"It is therefore necessary for a true physicist to always keep an open mind."

Dr. Moffet's final admonition, though couched in moderate terms, is, at the same time, in view of the era in which we live, a call to explore the far reaches of the universe, the infinite structure of matter, and the limitless borders of time.

The mystery of the Philadelphia Experiment has not yet been clarified, and its eventual answer may lie deep within the files of the Department of the Navy. Perhaps, as the Navy has so insistently contended, the entire incident is a legend and never took place. But then, considering the large amount of evidence that has been collected through the years, if the Philadelphia Experiment never happened as described, what actually *did* happen in a high-security area of the Philadelphia Navy Yard in October 1943?

Acknowledgments

The authors wish to express sincere thanks and appreciation to each of the following individuals and organizations, without whose help and encouragement it would have been impossible to write this book. In alphabetical order:

Dr. Som Agarwal—physicist, educator
Mike Akers—psychologist
Michelle Alberti—researcher
Janel Anderson—chemist
Janie Anderson—educator
Robert F. Anderson—educator
Carlos Miguel Allende
Mrs. P. Aponte-Allende
Gray Barker—author, publisher
Valerie Berlitz—author, artist
Lin Berlitz—researcher
Mrs. Ellis (Susan) Blockson—historian
T. Townsend Brown—physicist, inventor
Baron Johannes von Buttlar—author, UFO researcher
Reilly H. Crabb—researcher, lecturer, publisher

James V. Dalager, attorney at law

Mary B. D'Antonio—educator

James Davis, Jr.—computer sales

Mrs. Chrystal Dunninger

Frederick C. Durant III—director and curator, National Air and Space Museum

Helen Ellwood, LPN

Stanton T. Freedman—physicist, UFO researcher, author

Vincent Gaddis—author, researcher

Mrs. Anna Genslinger—researcher

Owen Heiberg—editor, journalist

Dr. Merle Hirsh—physicist, educator

Comdr. George W. Hoover, USN (retd.)

Robert Horning—student, photographer

Allen Huse—scientist

Dr. David M. Jacobs—historian, author

John A. Keel—author, researcher

Coral Lorenzen—author, UFO researcher

James Lorenzen—author, UFO researcher

Patrick Macey—researcher

Gary C. Magnuson—educator

Nic Magnuson—researcher

Dorothy M. Moore—archivist, historian

Duke Moore—artist

Lee Moore—computer programmer

Randy McIntosh—researcher, inventor

Otto Nathan—author, trustee of estate of Albert Einstein

Joan W. O'Connell—author, researcher

Dr. Linus Pauling—scientist, Nobel laureate

Lt. Col. Kenneth Peters, U.S.A. (Ret.)—military historian

Dr. Raymond A. Rossberg, M.D.

Sabina W. Sanderson—author, editor

Nate Singer—mentalist and psychic

Otto Alexander Steen—engineer, archivist, lecturer

Gene Steinberg—UFO researcher, writer

Harry Tokarz—president, CUFORN

Dr. J. Manson Valentine—oceanographer, archaeologist, explorer, cartographer

Bob Warth—research chemist; president, SITU

James R. Wolfe—author, researcher

John David Wood, president, Solarlogos, Inc.

Organizations:

The Aerial Phenomena Research Organization, Tucson, Ariz.

Borderland Sciences Research Foundation, Vista,
Calif.

Carnegie Library of Pittsburgh, Pa.

CUFORN, Inc., Willowdale, Ontario, Canada

Duquesne University Library, Pittsburgh, Pa.

The Einstein–Steen Sticks and Stones Museum &
Library, Tujunga, Calif.

The Herman Review, Herman, Minn.

Matson Navigation Company, San Francisco, Calif.

Minneapolis Public Library

Morris Public Library, Morris, Minn.

National Air and Space Museum, Smithsonian Institution, Washington, D.C.

National Archives, Washington, D.C.

The New York Times

National Investigations Committee on Aerial Phenomena, Kensington, Md.

Sewickley Public Library, Sewickley, Pa.

Society for the Investigation of the Unexplained,
Little Silver, N.J.

University of Michigan Library, Ann Arbor, Mich.

University of Minnesota Library, Morris, Minn.

U.S. Department of the Navy

U.S. Department of Commerce
Varo Corporation, Garland, Tex.

and the many others who have offered help, information, or encouragement, but who, for one reason
or another, must remain nameless in these pages.
Appreciation is especially directed to Robert Markel,
editor, whose prior interest in the Philadelphia Experiment was an important contribution to the publication of this book.

Chronological Bibliography

1947   Frank, Philip   *Albert Einstein, his Life and Times.* New York: Alfred Knopf, 1947.

1955   Jessup, M.K.   *The Case for the UFO.* Secaucus, N.J.: Citadel Press, 1955.

1957   Hlavaty, Vaclar   *Geometry of Einstein's Unified Field Theory.* Bloomington, Ind.: Indiana University Press, 1957.

1962   Crabb, Reilly H.   *M.K. Jessup, the Allende Letters and Gravity.* Vista, Calif.: BSRF Publications, 1962.

1963   Barker, Gray   *The Strange Case of Dr. M.K. Jessup.* Clarksburg, W. Va.: Saucerian Press, 1963.

1964   Gaddis, Vincent   *Invisible Horizons.* Philadelphia: Chilton Book Company, 1964.

1964   Barnothy, Madelene P. *The Effects of Magnetic Fields.* New York: Plenum Co., 1964

1967   Steiger, Brad   "Fantastic Key to the Flying Saucer Mystery," *Saga,* November 1967.

1967   Sanderson, Ivan T.   *Uninvited Visitors: A Biologist Looks at UFOs.* Chicago: Henry Regnery Co., 1967.

1968   Binder, Otto   *Flying Saucers are Watching Us.* New York: Tower Books, 1968, 1970.

1968   Sanderson, Ivan T.   "M.K. Jessup," *Pursuit,* September 30, 1968.

1968   O'Connell, Joan W., and Steiger, Brad   *New UFO Breakthrough.* New York: Award Books, 1968.

1969   Lorenzen, James, and Coral, Ed.   *A.P.R.O. Bulletin,* July-August 1969.

		Aerial Phenomena Research Organization, Tucson, Ariz.
1970	LePoer Trench, Brinsley	*Flying Saucers Have Arrived.* New York: World Publishing Co., 1970.
1971	Flammonde, Paris	*The Age of Flying Saucers.* New York: Hawthorne Books, 1971.
1973	Jessup, M.K. and Barker, Gray	*The Case for the UFO, Varo Annotated Edition,* facsimile. Clarksburg, W. Va.: Saucerian Press, 1973.
1973	von Buttlar, Johannes	*Journey to Infinity.* London: Wm. Collins Sons & Co., 1973.
1974	Salisbury, Dr. F.H.	*The Utah UFO Display.* Old Greenwich, Conn.: Devin-Adair, 1974.
1974	Sladek, Vincent	*The New Apocrypha.* New York: Stein & Day, 1974.
1974	Berlitz, Charles F.	*The Bermuda Triangle.* New York: Doubleday, 1974.
1975	Brennan, J.H.	*Beyond the 4th Dimension.* London:

		Futura Publications, 1975.
1975	Santesson, H.S.	"More on Jessup and the Allende Case," *Pursuit*, April 1975.
1976	Strong, B.R.	"The Allende Letters," *Official UFO*, April 1976.
1976	Elliott, A.	"Were the Allende Letters a College Prank?" *Pursuit*, April 1976.
1976	Cohen, Daniel	*Mysterious Disappearances*. New York: Dodd, Mead & Co., 1976.
1977	Berlitz, Charles F.	*Without a Trace*. New York: Doubleday, 1977.
1977	Jeffrey, Adi-Kent T.	*Parallel Universe*. New York: Warner Books, 1977.
1977	———	"New Evidence-Top Secret, Government-Alien Liaison?" *UFO Pulse Analyzer*, May 1977.
1977	Helms, Harry L., Jr.	"The Carlos Allende Letters, Key to the UFO Mystery?" *Argosy UFO Magazine*, Winter 1977–8.

1978   Simson, George E.,   *Thin Air*. New York:
            and Burger, Neal   Dell Publishing
            R.   Co., 1978. (Fiction)
1978   Barker, Gray, ed.   "Carlos Allende
                                    Speaks," tape.
                                    Clarksburg, W.
                                    Va.: Saucerian
                                    Press.
1978   Moore, William L.   "The Wizard of
                                    Electro-Gravity,"
                                    Saga UFO Report,
                                    May 1978. Excerpts
                                    used in this book
                                    by kind permission
                                    of Gambi
                                    Publications, Div.
                                    of Web Offset
                                    Industries,
                                    Brooklyn, N.Y.

Index